THE MYSTERIO
BROCKLE]

GENERAL GORDON'S
UNKNOWN AIDE

The Life of Major-General
John Fielden Brocklehurst
Lord Ranksborough
1852-1921

by Jean Bray

Published by
REARDON PUBLISHING
PO Box 919 Cheltenham, Glos, GL50 9AN Tel: 01242 231800
Website: www.reardon.co.uk Email: reardon@bigfoot.com

Copyright © 2006

ISBN 1 873877 77 3
9781873877777

Copyright Jean Bray © 2006

Cover Design Laurence Fish

Design & Layout Nicholas Reardon

Printed by Electric Ink Printing Company Ltd Gloucester

INTRODUCTION

Who was the young cavalry officer who became General Gordon's companion and was responsible for persuading Gordon to undertake his final mission to Khartoum?

His towering height was not matched by ambition but he rose to command a crack cavalry regiment and, without the advantages of birth or wealth became the trusted friend and confidant of two Queens of England.

How did he manage so successfully to combine a position in the Royal household and work with the radical crusading journalist WT Stead on diplomatic missions to resolve the Boer War and attempt to introduce democracy to Russia before the revolution.? Yet his name and adventures remain unrecorded in any of the history books of his era.

For the first time we have been able to access his private papers and those of his family to reveal the hitherto unknown cavalryman who was to play such an important role behind the scenes in many of the major events of his lifetime.

ACKNOWLEDGEMENTS

This book is based mainly on the Ranksborough Papers and my greatest debt of gratitude is to Johnny Van Haeften who not only gave me permission to use this previously unpublished material but also much time and enthusiastic support both during my research and towards this publication.

I would also particularly like to thank Lady Ashcombe for her encouragement and support, for allowing me to use the Sudeley Castle archives and for creating an exhibition and film/DVD 'Letters to Khartoum' based on an episode from the book which is now showing at the Castle.

One of the greatest pleasures in researching this book has been the people I have met unexpectedly on the way - of these the most important has been Gerald Stewart of Pocono Pines, Pennsylvania. A chance browsing on the internet led me to Gerald who, with his wife Enola, is working on a new complete Gordon Bibliography.

This is a remarkable work which comprises more than 20,000 individual pages covering more than 2000 titles. Jerry was immediately enthusiastic about my book and became my friend and mentor. I owe so much to his support and advice- from editing my manuscript - to sourcing rare books, references and people and giving me endless encouragement. I shall miss his four in the morning e-mails.

I wish to acknowledge the permission of Her Majesty Queen Elizabeth II to quote from the Journal of Queen Victoria and other material in the Royal Archives and to use Queen Alexandra's letters to John Brocklehurst in the Ranksborough Papers. I am particularly grateful to Miss Allison Derrett the Assistant Registrar of the Royal Archives for transcribing Queen Alexandra's letters for me and for her valuable interest and help.

I am most grateful to General Gordon's joint copyright holders - Mr David Gordon and Mr John Bell for their permission to use General Gordon's letters to John Brocklehurst in the Ranksborough Papers. I very much enjoyed meeting Mr David Gordon when he came to the opening of the related exhibition and film at Sudeley Castle.

Gerald Stewart helped me to find the distinguished American writer and historian Joseph O Baylen and I would like to thank Mr Baylen very much for permission to quote from his published material on Brocklehurst's friend WT Stead relating to the Boer War and the Romanov family.

Brocklehurst's Rutland connections were explored in a visit to Langham and I am most grateful to Lil Walker for her hospitality and for introducing me to her friends Audrey Hubbard, Margaret Catchpole and Benjie Walker with memories of Lord Ranksborough. I am especially grateful to Lil for her permission to use extracts from the diary of her brother Ernest Walker. I would also like to thank Tim Clough the Honorary Editor of the 'Rutland Review' - the journal of the Rutland Local History and Record Society - for publishing my article on Lord Ranksborough.

By good fortune this article came to the attention of historian and author Henry Keown-Boyd who became intrigued by the story of the Curtis letters and led to my meeting and involvement with the Melik Society. I would like to thank Henry particularly for reading my manuscript .and for his very helpful corrections, comments and suggestions.

The Rev Dr John Pollock author of 'Gordon - the Man Behind the Legend' very kindly introduced me to the Gordon copyright holders and has given me every encouragement in getting my book published.

I would also like to thank the following who contributed to my research: Mr K C Hughes, Assistant Curator of The Household Cavalry Museum: Jonathan Swift, Manuscript Cataloguer at Trinity College Library, Cambridge: and Rusty MacLean, Librarian and Archivist at Rugby School.

I have been very fortunate to have had practical help, advice and encouragement from   Major-General Barney White-Spunner who made use of my then unpublished mss in his book Horse Guards: historian and writer Beau Riffenbergh; writer and broadcaster Fergus Nicoll, historian and writer David Donaldson who helped with proof-reading; and David Morris for introducing us to our printer.

My special thanks to my husband, Laurence for his encouragement, enthusiasm and patience as well as for the cover design, and to Nicholas Reardon for finally making it all happen.

CHAPTER ONE

Among the handful of final letters which General Gordon sent out from the siege of Khartoum was one to his 'dear friend' Brocklehurst. A decade earlier they had met in Cairo where the young cavalry officer had arrived to shoot big game and found himself instead becoming Gordon's chosen travelling companion.

"Johnny is at Cairo waiting to join an expedition to Abyssinia", his aunt Emma Dent recorded in her diary at Sudeley Castle .in February 1877 - "Colonel Gordon is at Cairo - he is made Governor of the Soudan, absolute and uncontrolled - the Soudan is supposed to mean from the second cataract as far as anyone can go, South and West, a country larger than England and crossed in every direction by slave dealers, whose destruction is his great object in life - an expedition perilous though glorious.

Colonel Gordon has taken an immense fancy to Johnny and wishes to get leave of absence for him for 12 months from the Duke of Cambridge, to whom he has telegraphed for the same."

He had also taken "a great liking" to Emma's sister, Marianne and her friend Mary Booth, who were also in Cairo. Marianne described him as a very gentle, quiet, dreamy little man - apt to go off into reveries. "He said almost inaudibly 'I do not know how they will like me those people in the Soudan, the part I have been governing is not a sixth the size, however they gave me no trouble' and he smiled gently and was gone off again in a reverie - and this is the great Leviathan who led one half of China against the other half to victory."

At the time Charles Gordon was already famous, having served with great bravery in the Crimean War and led the Ever Victorious Army through its hazardous adventures in helping to suppress the Taiping Rebellion in China.

He had just spent an exhausting two and a half years as Governor of the Equatoria Province on the Upper Nile - mapping and exploring the river, driving out the Arab slave traders and setting up a dozen military forts, forming a connecting chain of settlements for 600 miles. Worn out by the unbearable heat and disillusioned by his own success he resigned the job - writing to his sister Augusta,"I have a sort of wish that I will get rid of Colonel Gordon".

However, others were more encouraged by his success. The Khedive Ismail, who ruled Egypt at the time, had been one of his admirers and when Egypt needed someone to administer the Sudan - collect taxes, come to terms with Abyssinia and keep the peace generally, he decided to call for Gordon's return.

On 17th January 1877 he telegraphed to Gordon in London: "I refuse to believe that once Gordon has given his word as a gentleman anything will ever induce him to go back on it": signed Your affectionate Ismail.

As a result of this Gordon decided to return to Cairo in February 1877 and named his terms to the Khedive - he must have the governor-generalship of the whole Sudan - nearly a million square miles. He also demanded full powers to parley with the Negus of Abyssinia and to suppress the slave trade.

"Then I began and told him all; and then he gave me the Soudan and I leave on Saturday morning", he wrote. True to his usual modesty he halved the salary for the post - from £6,000 to £3,000 a year.

By this time Cairo was enjoying boom conditions. Since the opening of the Suez Canal a great influx of Western officials and tourists had begun to transform the Egyptian capital into a modern city. It was full of 'collectors on the scent of papyri and ruins, men of science with scientific ends in view, artists in search of subjects and invalids in search of health.' Thomas Cook had already opened offices there for tourists who wanted to journey down the Nile.

There were also plenty of adventurous young men - eager to shoot crocodiles or make expeditions into the interior.

Among them was a young officer in the Blues called Johnny Brocklehurst. He stood out from the rest with his great height and luxuriant cavalry moustache, but it was his ready wit and uninhibited high spirits which attracted him to Gordon. Seldom had he met with such enthusiasm. He easily persuaded Brocklehurst to forego his hunting trip and go with him to Abyssinia and although the Household Cavalry would not release Brocklehurst to join Gordon's staff he was soon to become his close friend and aide.

***

It is a long way from the Sudan to Macclesfield where Johnny Brocklehurst was born on the 13th May 1852 - the eldest son of Henry Brocklehurst and Ann Fielden, whose marriage in May 1848 cemented an alliance of two of the Victorian era's most successful trading dynasties.

The relationship between the two families began when their respective fathers, John Brocklehurst and John Fielden were both elected as Members of Parliament in the Reform Parliament of 1832 and became close friends. The two men had much in common. Although both were very successful businessmen they lived simple and unostentatious lives and John Brocklehurst in particular was keen on the avoidance of 'creeping luxuries'.

Macclesfield had been a centre for the silk trade since the end of the 18th century, and with the advent of the machine age the weaving of broad silk increased, dye houses were created and silk in all its varieties was prepared for the twister and weaver. The Brocklehursts were the largest silk millers in the town, employing more than 8,000 hands at the height of their prosperity.

John Brocklehurst, Henry's father, made the import of raw silk for the throwing mills his special study and he protested vigorously, both in and out of Parliament, when the advent of Free Trade in 1832 threatened the future of the Macclesfield mills. Later, when the silk trade was in the doldrums in the middle of the 19th century, and many mills were being closed down as a result, he spent £70,000 of his own money to keep his mills going and his workforce from starving - saying that he had made his money in Macclesfield and if need be he would spend it all there - down to his last sixpence.

He held his Parliamentary seat for the town for 36 years "earnestly promoting both there and elsewhere the interests of his fellow-townsmen and of his workpeople". During this time he had served under three Prime Ministers, Melbourne, Palmerston and Lord John Russell - "twice declining the Honours offered by his Queen, desiring no other satisfaction than to do his Duty."

While the Brocklehursts were kings of the silk trade the Fieldens headed the cotton trade. John Fielden's family enterprise - the Fielden Brothers of Todmorden - accumulated more capital in business than any other cotton firm in Britain in the time before the American Civil War, and by the next generation the Fieldens were among the wealthiest nouveaux riches in Victorian England.

However, they shared the same paternal patriarchal style of management as the Brocklehursts, believing that the well-being of their Todmorden labour force was essential to the firm's prosperity. John Fielden during the time he was MP for Oldham championed the causes of the handloom weavers and the working poor and played a leading part in securing the passage of the Ten Hours Bill through Parliament. He lost his Parliamentary seat in 1847, splitting his Radical supporters by choosing John Morgan Cobbett as his running partner; Cobbett then being regarded as a Tory.

The friendship between John Brocklehurst and John Fielden soon led to their families meeting and mixing and when John Brocklehurst's daughter, Emma, married John Coucher Dent of Sudeley Castle in September 1847 she chose Ann Fielden, John Fielden's second daughter as one of her bridesmaids. "She was a most charming, fascinating girl", Emma wrote in her diary many years later -"but in some ways delicate and now I can remember certain habits of indolence and indulgence, encouraged by the doctor, which led in her after life to much sorrow and mischief.

Then she was the best of us all - of course one of my bridesmaids and after our wedding she remained the longest at Hurdsfield - the family home. Then our poor dear Henry lost his heart - he was so handsome and warmhearted and gay - no one could have refused him, much less Ann Fielden - so the son and daughter of two old friends became engaged."

We learn later that Henry proposed to Ann at Hever Castle and they were married in May 1848 at Todmorden. The two families could not have been more pleased if it had been an arranged marriage rather than a love match. Unfortunately for us, as she would have described it well, Emma was still honey-mooning in Europe when the wedding took place, but we know that Brocklehursts came to Todmorden from Macclesfield ' in strength' for the occasion, staying at Centre Vale (John Fielden's house) and indeed filling all the other Fielden houses in the neighbourhood.

After the birth of a daughter, Marianne, who became known as Maimie, Henry and Ann's eldest son, John Fielden Brocklehurst, was born on the 13th May 1852. He was named John after both his grandfathers, although the family always called him Johnny.

His father was now a partner in the family silk milling business and at first all seemed well with the young family, but by the time that their fourth son was born in 1861 Ann's continual ill health was beginning to put a strain on their relationship. She was also reputedly "in a great state of mind" owing to Johnny having been sent to Macclesfield Free Grammar School at the age of nine.

Returning from a holiday in Europe in 1862 Henry's sister, Emma Dent, wrote in her diary - "I went to Stanhope Terrace - their London house - in the hope of doing something to reconcile Henry and his wife who are living on wretched terms - at the end of some days and many confabulations Sam Fielden [Ann's brother] made them shake hands and promise to make a fresh start, but as Ann herself says she fears she is incapable of making him happy or of doing all she ought to do as wife and mother."

Presumably the reconciliation worked on this first occasion, as the following year, 1863, Henry was Mayor of Macclesfield, when the whole town celebrated the wedding of the Prince of Wales to "the fair Alexandra of Denmark".

March 10th was the Royal Wedding Day and Emma Dent, who had gone home to Macclesfield for the occasion, reports that the day dawned "bright and clear - the hills covered with snow - but an east wind to show to advantage the innumerable flags and banners floating from windows, church towers and factories.

My father and I shared with Mrs Meek her window at the top of Hibel Road and had a good view of the procession - Henry at the head as Mayor. It was a wonderful procession consisting of yeomanry, 1600 children, clubs, clergy etc. It took an hour and a half to pass. We then went to the Parks where all assembled in an enormous circle and sang God Save the Queen with additional verses. The Rifle Corps then went thro' different manoeuvres, saluting the Mayor etc. and then all dispersed till evening when Henry's ball was given in the Town Hall for about 350 of the most respectable inhabitants of the Town - the following evening another ball was given to about 400 of the juveniles - a very pretty sight it was."

"We can only hope she will have a good husband", Emma mused about the Royal couple, "as he alone can make her happy and tho' she may have the heart of all England her home will not be a happy one unless he is good and kind." How amazed she would have been had she known that some 35 years later her nephew Johnny would become part of their Royal household. In the meantime his parents, still amicably together again were invited to a Grand Ball at the Mansion House in London which the Prince and Princess attended "and they danced and enjoyed themselves like any other young things."

However, the truce in their marriage did not last. Within a couple of years Emma found Henry in a "very low bad way indeed - he quite alarmed me. He has struggled on for so many years with his poor unfortunate wife that at last his own health is giving way".

Doctors advised change - going abroad and absence from home - which Henry took and went to Italy although leaving an unhappy house, "full of the misery Ann has brought upon them all by her tempers and lack of common sense".

Soon after this they separated, Ann and the two youngest children living in their London house in Stanhope Gate while Henry remained in Macclesfield. Probably as a result of the separation he decided to send the three older boys, Johnny, Harry and Alfred to boarding school. Why he chose Rugby we do not know - there were no family connections with the school, nor with any of the other public schools.

Johnny arrived at Rugby School just before his fifteenth birthday in May 1867 and the other two followed him there. Frederick Temple was Headmaster and Johnny was just in time for the 300th birthday of the school which was celebrated on the 26th June 1867 with much ceremony; beginning with a service in the Chapel and ending with a dinner chaired by Dean Stanley and held in the Town Hall where a gallery was specially erected to accommodate the ladies among the 200 guests. They had to sit through 19 speeches, including one from Dean Stanley who said at the Third Cataract of the Nile he had 'rejoiced to see how large a proportion of Rugby names were carved on the rock which marked the southern extremity of European travel.'

Johnny Brocklehurst's time at Rugby was undistinguished. School records show that he boarded in Wilson's House (now known as Whitelaw House) and his tutor was Arthur Sidgwick, who was later Tutor at Corpus Christi. He won no prizes and was not in any of the sports teams but there is a record of him being an unenrolled member of Rugby School in the 12th Warwickshire Rifle Volunteers.

The only glimpse we have of his schooldays is 35 years later - in August 1902 - when acting as the King's Understudy for the full dress rehearsal of Edward VII's Coronation at Westminster Abbey he enlivened the rather solemn and decorous occasion by joking, after receiving the homage of the Archbishop of Canterbury, Dr Temple, that the last time he had come into personal contact with that great man was when he had received a flogging at his hands at Rugby, some 35 years earlier.

Rugby School records have no mention of the flogging or the reason for it, but it seems likely that he must have committed a serious offence or breaking of the rules to have merited a flogging from the headmaster.

Then in his last year at Rugby he was devastated by the sudden death of his father in January 1870. Although Henry had been fighting ill-health for some time, much of it the result of his difficult marriage, the suddenness of his death was a terrible shock, particularly as Johnny's mother was ill in London and he was left to take responsibiliby for the family - collecting his two brothers Harry and Alfred from Rugby to pay their respects to their dead father before journeying with them to London to comfort their mother.

The rest of the Brocklehurst family gathered at Macclesfield, where Emma went upstairs to see Henry - "looking so grand and peaceful in his last sleep - poor fellow - all his troubles over."

Several thousand people lined the three miles of road between Macclesfield and Prestbury for the funeral procession. "Not only did the inhabitants of the town pour forth to witness the mournful procession", reported the local paper, "But all employed in the mills, from the highest to the lowest joined in sharing their last respect to their beloved friend and master." All the mill girls spent a portion of their weekly earnings buying crepe and black rosettes to wear on their bonnets and ignored the rain and cold of the January morning to line the route.

"The flag hung at half mast high on the old Town Hall and when the procession arrived at Prestbury it was met by members of the various municipal bodies of the town, including the Macclesfield Corporation and the Fire Brigade, of which since its formation Henry had been the Captain. The bell of the Parish Church pealed its muffled toll and all were hushed in silence as the procession neared the Church; here the members of the Corporation, the managers, the tradesmen and friends, formed into line from the Church to the road and the coffin was slowly borne along the avenue thus formed. No greater tribute of respect could be paid to a man than for those who had formerly been employed by him to come forward and bear personal testimony to the respect in which he was held. "A further tribute listed his achievements in helping to shorten the hours of labour in the silk mills and warehouses - to ensure cleanliness and health in the factories - to establish a school of design and to enlarge and support the Mechanics Institute in Macclesfield… "A good father, a judicious master, an excellent townsman and a true patriot" was his epitaph.

Johnny, who was in London with his mother, had to miss the funeral, but returned to Macclesfield as soon as he could, only underlining his father's enforced exile from his home in

London - "how Henry had intended to see his wife but could not face her - what an agony it had cost him to pass his own door, longing to see his little children, yet dreading to see his wretched wife."

None of his four sons were to follow their father into the silk mills. Johnny and Harry were both keen horsemen and determined to join the elite Household Cavalry. A generation earlier this would have seemed impossible, but wealth and education had opened many doors for the families of successful trades people, even though the Royal Horse Guards - the Blues - Johnny's regiment of choice still remained largely the province of the aristocracy. In 1899 of its 25 serving officers seven were peers and six the sons of peers. Fortunately the reform and modernisation of the Army by Edward Cardwell, Gladstone's Secretary of State for War, had recently led to the abolition of the purchase of commissions.

Instead of going to Staff College Johnny decided to go to Cambridge, on the understanding that a degree would be sufficient qualification to gain him a commission in the Guards. With the help of a 'crammer' he was admitted to Trinity College, Cambridge from Rugby in July 1870, although it sounds as if he just scraped in, as he was placed one from the bottom in a class of nine in his first year College examination.

The same month the family were in mourning again, with the death of their mother on the 19th July 1870, six months after her husband, almost as if having plagued Henry through life she was determined to pursue him beyond the grave.

This left Johnny, now aged 18, as the head of the orphaned family, as his elder sister Maimie was already happily married to Gibbon Worthington. The two youngest children, Ernest then aged 9 and Constance (Annie) aged 7 went to live with Ann's brother, John Fielden at Dobroyd Castle. He had no children of his own and they were virtually brought up by him, leaving Johnny, Harry and Alfred to be absorbed by the Brocklehursts, particularly by their indomitable Brocklehurst aunts, Emma and Marianne.

CHAPTER TWO

Bad news of Johnny at Trinity College, Cambridge - playing high" his Aunt Emma recorded in her diary in April 1873. "A good letter from Mr Blore [his tutor] on the subject. He has promised not to play any more while he remains there".

It seems unlikely that Brocklehurst's gambling would have resulted in his being sent down. Such a matter would have been dealt with first by his tutor and would only come before the Master and Seniors of the college if this failed. In any case he was close to taking his degree which Cambridge records show was not an honours degree, but "an ordinary degree which allowed for little specialisation in a mainly general series of examinations." Family records say that he was "going in for" English History, so it seems probable that he took the Law and History special paper, sitting for the ordinary BA in 1873.

In the meantime, while the family elders considered that he was "inclined to be not a little bit wild" Johnny himself declared that he intended to be "a pride and comfort to his family instead of a Black Sheep".

However, he was soon in trouble again. This time with the Cheshire Militia "for having deserted his militia duty for five days without having reported himself". The family were very concerned that this would be counted against him when he joined the Army. To which he replied that having got through his degree very well and having resigned the militia he thought it was not necessary to appear at all. What did upset him was to find that his degree at Cambridge, which was supposed to have been sufficient to get him his commission in the Army, did not replace the Army exams and he was sent to work for these at Canterbury with one of Lord Leigh's sons under some good coach.

At last, on the 2nd December 1874 Brocklehurst, aged 22, gained his commission in the Blues and was entered as a full lieutenant.

Soon after that he spent a few days at Sudeley Castle on his way to Badminton. "A curious and somewhat interesting specimen of the Tribe of the Royal Horse Guards", his Aunt Emma described him in her diary. "Clothes superlative - boots, oh ye gods what fits. What expanse of shirt front when dressed for dinner - how careful at dinner not to partake of fattening food - I was afraid he was not well, but his Uncle Dent said 'it was only d----- affectation!' The expression of the young guardsman's face thereupon was a study. We had some discussions on 'women' and how they should be treated with all honesty by these smart young men - afterwards he wrote from Badminton "I w'd not tarry ten minutes on this sublunary sphere if the petticoats were to quit - Did not your father used to say 'There never was an ugly woman'? By my halidam I agree with him."

With no children of her own Emma enjoyed being a favourite and generous aunt. In particular she made Johnny an annual allowance of £1,000 a year during his time in the Army. Regimental life in the cavalry at the time could cost as much as

£600 to £1,000 a year to pay for mess bills (which frequently exceeded an officer's pay) as well as the many subscriptions, uniforms and equipment. However, having married not just a husband but also a castle, she was mostly too thoroughly immersed in the history and community of Sudeley and Winchcombe to spend too much time away from Sudeley with her nephews.

It was her younger sister Marianne who introduced Johnny to the desert, and ultimately to Charles Gordon, later Gordon of Khartoum. Marianne was the youngest of John Brocklehurst's children - 10 years younger than Emma - and was prettier and wittier than her sister. She was still only a teenager when their mother died and she remained at home with her father who was determined that she would marry well. In this respect Marianne evaded his best efforts. "She had many admirers, three of them were clever and desirable in every way - so much so that my Father ventured on one occasion to urge the propriety of well weighing her decision" said her sister. Marianne took this for something stronger and sent Emma an allegorical drawing of her father pushing his 'Dinah' down the precipice of matrimony at the bottom of which was the sea of her future life with sundry little boats thereon. "The future for me, well never mind I am not ready yet and I won't be pushed into anything." she wrote.

"Three of her suitors are now baronets" Emma noted - "which shows how she was esteemed - but she was not for marrying and they were all allowed to pass on without any hesitation on her part."

Then she fell in love. Henry Coventry wooed her well and seemed eminently suitable - but her father, John Brocklehurst would not hear of the match. "His objections were not only on the score of want of property but that the Coventry family generally were not such as he would have his daughter marry into - even the present young Earl is already so much on the Turf!", reported Emma. "Nothing we can say has any effect - he is perfectly hard and obdurate and has refused to see Henry Coventry at all." To Emma's great surprise and dismay Marianne gave in to her father's wishes and broke off her engagement

From that time she turned her back on marriage and began to enjoy her increasing freedom to travel. She took up photography, which was then in its infancy, and acquired a partner, Mary Booth, who was to become her friend and lifelong companion. For some time Marianne had been signing herself MB and with the addition of Mary Booth they were to become known both in and outside the family as the MBs. "Marianne and Miss Booth seem so all in all to one another", Emma observed.

Like many Victorian women of that time the MBs became fascinated by the desert and in the winter of 1873 they set off for the Nile taking with them Johnny's younger brother,18-year-old Alfred and George their groom. On the crossing from Brindisi they met the writer Amelia B Edwards, who was to describe them later in her book "A Thousand Miles Up the Nile", as two English ladies "of whom we have seen so much ever since that we regard them by this time as quite old friends in a strange land."

Since the opening of the Suez Canal Cairo had become a hub for travellers to the East. John Murray had already published a guide to Egypt and by the time the MB's arrived there Thomas Cook had opened tourist offices for those "who wanted to explore the Ancient River under British management."

This involved hiring a dahabeeyah - described by Amelia Edwards as 'not very unlike the Noah's Ark of our childhood', shallow and flat-bottomed, adapted for sailing or rowing, with cabins on deck and a raised 'open-air drawing room'. After the MBs and Amelia Edwards and her party had hired their respective boats - the Philae and the Bagstones, the latter re-named after the MB's house at Swythamley - together with appropriate crew, they entered into a solemn convention to start together, moor together and keep together all the way up the Nile. "This social compact was carried out as far as Abu Simbel; that is to say during a period of seven weeks hard going and for a distance of upwards 800 miles", wrote Amelia Edwards.

She was particularly amused by George, the MB's groom "whom they had brought out from the wilds of Lancashire, partly because he is a good shot and may be useful to Master Alfred after birds and crocodiles; and partly from a well-founded belief in his general abilities.

And George, who is a fellow of infinite jest and infinite resource, takes to the Egyptian life as a duckling to the water. He picks up Arabic as if it were his mother tongue. He skins birds like a practised taxidermist. He can wash and iron on occasion. He is in short groom, footman, housemaid, laundry maid, stroke, oar, gamekeeper and general factotum all in one. And besides all this he is gifted with a comic gravity of countenance that no suprises and no disasters can upset for a moment. To see this worthy anachronism cantering along in his groom's coat and gaiters, livery buttons, spotted neckcloth, tall hat and all the rest of it; his long legs dangling within an inch of the ground on either side of the most diminutive of donkeys; his double-barrelled fowling piece under his arm, and that imperturbable look in his face, one would have sworn that he and Egypt were friends of old, and that he had been brought up on pyramids from his earliest childhood".

The two boats sailed down the Nile to the second cataract where they were shocked to find that people had carved their names on the rock - no doubt similar to the Rugby names which Dean Stanley had discovered at the third cataract. For the return journey the big sails of the dahabeeyah were taken down and the boats turned into a galley for the rowers, with only one small sail remaining.

On this return journey Marianne and Alfred shot one or two crocodiles and at Minya the MBs took the train to Cairo, leaving Alfred and George the groom to complete the journey by boat. From Cairo the MB's went on to Palestine and Syria aboard the Messagerie steamer "La Bourdonnais", and when they returned to England in 1874 they took the curiosities they had discovered on their travels to the British Museum where they were all pronounced "genuine".

They declared Cairo to be the most enchanting city in the world and, still full of enthusiasm for the desert, they returned to Egypt in 1877. This time it was Johnny who accompanied them.

He was just recovering from a serious hunting accident in which he fell into a ditch with his horse landing on top of him. Reports from the hunting field said he would have been killed but for the happy suggestion of a young farmer who said "get a saddle off one of the horses and strap it on the gentleman's head." When this was done they were able to move the horse from over him where they lay in the ditch together - the horse naturally struggled violently and the saddle was cut to pieces. "Five gentlemen rode back to the rescue and jumped the fence to get to him, but the whole five could not have saved him but for this clever thought which had never entered anybody's head before".

In Cairo the MB's and Johnny met Charles Gordon, who had just arrived there to take up his appointment as Governor-General of the Sudan. The Sudan at the time covered nearly a million square miles. It was "a vast and undefined region stretching south of Egypt to the Equator. The greater part of it is desert and although its area exceeds that of India its population is not three times that of the State of New York" The Sudanese were a mixed race - an intermingling of Arabs with the black indigenous tribes and apart from some pagan negroes on the Nile they were Moslems.

There were no towns of any size except Khartoum which was situated at the juncture of the two Niles and El Obeid, the capital of Kordofan. The only transport was by boats on the Nile or caravans of camels and mules in the desert and the only outside link was the new telegraph line from Khartoum to Cairo.

"The Egyptian government in the Sudan was a mere matter of periodical pillage, accompanied by the torture of men and the rapings of women. Its only redeeming feature was that it prevented internecine wars. The system of government was essentially Turkish."

When Gordon accepted his appointment as Governor-General, at the Khedive Ismail's request he warned him that this would be fatal to the continuance of this old system. "Never more will Egypt be able to govern the Soudan in the old Turkish or Circassian fashion after I have resided there long enough to teach the people that they have rights" he said. "If you send me you must continue my system or lose the Soudan".

When Gordon left his successor reverted to the old system, with the result that Gordon had predicted - Egypt lost the Sudan - which is why he later proclaimed "I have laid the egg which the Mahdi has hatched. I taught the people they had rights. Everything has sprung from that".

In that February of 1877 his task in the Sudan was only just beginning, and in Cairo he was amused to meet the MBs -two English women who were not taking advantage of the luxuries of Shepheard's Hotel but camping in the desert with their tents and camels. For some reason he jokingly christened them "the Foreign Office" and from then on he always referred to them in this way.

He also took a particular liking to Johnny Brocklehurst. The young cavalry officer was taking advantage of his annual leave to see something of foreign lands, as members of the Household Cavalry seldom had the chance to serve overseas. He was in Egypt to find adventure or to shoot crocodile. Gordon's first task as Governor-General was to go to the Red Sea coast and then up-country to Abyssinia, to try and make a deal with King John. He invited Brocklehurst to accompany him, and telegraphed to the Duke of Cambridge with the request to grant Brocklehurst 12 months leave of absence from the Royal Horse Guards.

Hoping that this would be granted, they set out together in the Egyptian frigate which had been put at Gordon's disposal and became great friends during the voyage to Massawa in the part of Eritrea which at that time belonged to the Sudan. It might have seemed an unlikely friendship between the young cavalry officer and the God-fearing Puritan soldier but Gordon had a great gift for friendship. They soon discovered that they shared the same values and the same jokes and Johnny

Brocklehurst, who had been orphaned at the age of 18, found in Charles Gordon the adult influence and example which had been missing from his life up to that time.

CHAPTER THREE

One of His Highness transports had just returned into harbour with 400 troops from Massowah and 40 Krupp steel guns. The ship was burned and the whole cargo of guns destroyed." read a newspaper report on the Khedive's campaign in Abyssinia. "A young gentleman named Brocklehurst is said to have behaved very gallantly and was nearly drowned".

Brocklehurst himself described the incident in a letter to his Uncle Peter: "I went to Abyssinia with Colonel Gordon to make peace with King John, but being unable to get far inland owing to the disturbances and as my application for 12 months leave to accompany Gordon had been refused, I left him and was hurrying back to Suez in a man o'war the *'Latif'*, laden with soldiers and gunpowder, to join a slaving expedition just starting down the Red Sea under McKillip Pasha, when we were burnt about 100 miles from Suez. It was a horrible scene and beyond my powers of description, very near proving advantageous to my 'heir apparent' and making mine very much so, but thanks to a British India ship the *'Agra'* I saved my skin and a pair of flannel trousers."

An even more detailed account of events was later given by his Aunt Emma. "En route to Grenoble who should turn up but Johnny, travelling back to London - his leave of absence being up on April 24." she recorded "He was looking out of his carriage window and discovered the back of Uncle Dent's head - he looked further and discovered the owner thereof in the extremely round person in the celebrated enormous topcoat which hides our little fox terrier in the sleeve - more remarkable on that day the heat being excessive and equal to July in England.

He travelled in our carriage for an hour when we extracted a few more particulars of his adventures. He spoke in enthusiastic terms of Colonel Gordon, with whom he would dearly have liked to join in his Egyptian Expedition. It was after accompanying him to Abyssina, he not having been able to reach the court of King John owing to the disturbed state of the country, that he was hurrying back down the Red Sea when the ship took fire.

The alarm was in the night - he rushed up on deck where the smoke was rising up in thick clouds - the troops were screaming and praying - panic seized alike the Egyptian soldiers and officers - discipline was not thought of.

The flames soon divided the ship into two parts - so that the people on board were also divided - a rush was made for the boats - too few to hold half - ropes were cut and the boats upset - many fell into the water, which fortunately was calm, but the effect of the struggling Egyptians in the water, clearer than day owing to the phosphorescent light, was too ghastly to be imagined or described.

An English Indian ship the *'Agra'* appeared but the *'Latif'* was going at her full speed - no-one in the engine room to guide or stay her - the engineer was an Englishman and seeing the only chance of safety was to lessen or stop the speed he made one more effort to reach the engine room - where the fire had started - and succeeded in stopping her.

In the meantime Johnny was in the hinder part of the ship - the flames and the heat rapidly striding up on him. He found a small boat there which he lowered and into which the men dropped - he the last. He stood up amid them and with a thick stick struck on head or knuckles those who moved, or struggled to get into the boat, which was already half full of water. So by calm determination he got them safely up to the *'Agra'* when they could no longer contain themselves and sprang like cats at the ropes, very nearly upsetting the boat. Johnny did not get on board with them and was going back to rescue others, when seeing his small boat rapidly filling he jumped into the water and swam for the *'Agra'* which steamed off just as he reached her. His heart sank a little within him and he was just thinking how best to reserve his strength when the joyful sound of the splash of oars told him help was at hand.

The passengers on board were all kindness itself and a small man with a large heart rigged him out in his clothes for he had saved nothing - and owing to the gunpowder on board the *'Latif'* and the guns firing as the fire reached them it was too dangerous to make the attempt."

In a report on the circumstances of the affair to the British India Steam Navigation Company the captain of the *'Agra'* Captain C H Hillcoat said that the *'Latif'* being a wooden vessel had burnt rapidly and was enveloped in flames from end to end half an hour before the last boat quitted her side. Her guns being loaded, went off at intervals and the explosions from time to time were extremely dangerous to the safety of the different boats' crews. The steamer *'Myra'* also carried some 30 soldiers and more would have been lost but for the utter want to discipline among the Egyptian troops. They swamped one boat by jumping into her by dozens and the men of the *'Agra'* in the other boats had to use their oars and stretchers to hook them off or they would have been lost also. The disaster took place several miles from shore. The night was clear and the sea was smooth."

Brocklehurst not only lost all his luggage and possessions but also Gordon's tunic and sword and dress clothes which he was taking back to England. He wired Gordon immediately on his return who wrote; "I was truly glad to hear of your escape....It will have made you think much of our conversation on death, etc....Believe me my dear Brocklehurst, rejoicing that God has designed you for more work on earth."

Another letter followed a week later: "I hope you got home safe, what a terrible disaster for you, I hope you did not lose anything you could not replace. I have had no details, Fowler's rifle and Esterhezy's hunting knife and my beautiful tunic and sword and dress clothes!!! I have not broken my heart over them".

Gordon by this time had managed to move into the interior and had arrived at Keren where he summoned "the redoubtable brigand Walad-el-Michael and got him to accept a government away from the Frontier. "I treated him very well" he wrote to Brocklehurst, "but it is a sad business, for he was a scoundrel to betray his country and religion. People are terribly afraid of him, and he was quite strong enough to have taken me and the Fort, if he had liked. I ate the humble pie, but did not like the taste".

"Do you see to what address I have written, ha! ha!" he joked, having sent the letter to Brocklehurst at the Officer's Guard Room at the War Office. "24 hrs solitary confinement - well, perhaps it is better than these lands." He sent his regards to the MBs and told Brocklehurst to see Lieutenant Watson RE, "who lives near the Guard room, up the small staircase on the left, as you enter your den."

Having still failed to make contact with King John of Abyssinia, who was away fighting a rival, Gordon then set out on one of his legendary journeys by mule and camel to reach Kassala on the Atbara river.

"I have had lots of bother and worries", he told Brocklehurst in his next letter. "Affairs with Johannis [King John] and Walad-el-Michael are by no means in a settled state. Johannis is hard pressed by the attack of Menelik, who has a large force with him, and, who, I expect will find John some occupation.

"I hate this country and its ways, but this is no use, and I must go through with it. I go to Darfur when I have done with this work, and thence to Silia or to Berbera.

"Goodbye my dear Brocklehurst. Do not be ambitious, if you would be happy, be content with the lot into which you are thrown", he advised.

Gordon continued to follow the great trade route from the Atbara river and then went by boat down the Nile to Khartoum where he was ceremonially installed as Governor-General on 5 May 1877 in front of an enthusiastic crowd.

He lost no time in setting about improving the situation there "sending out a stream of new statutes and decrees that were aimed at breaking up the power of the officials and making life more bearable for the poor. Flogging in the prisons was abolished, taxes on peasants lightened or remitted altogether and a box for petitions set up at the Palace door, while the worst of the army officers and civil servants were sent packing to Cairo".

As a result trade flowed again and Khartoum began to look more like a modern city although Gordon was seldom there to enjoy it. Before the end of May he set out to suppress the revolt in the western province of Darfur - some 97 days of camel riding away.

He had soon become a prodigious camel traveller, even fabled to outride the Bedouin. Gordon himself joked that "the Gordons and camels are of the same race - take an idea into their heads and nothing will take it out".

"I am in a mess here" he wrote to Brocklehurst in June from Oom Changa (Um Shanga) in Darfur. "I want to concentrate my troops to make head against the revolt, and I have the greatest difficulty in doing so. However there is an end to all things and I shall d.v. get out of this mess....
"I will write again soon and hope you will get strong and well. I am very very uncomfortable, the heat is terrible and I have no end of bothers. Why was I ambitious?"

Darfur continued to be the main source of trouble. In 1874 a Sudanese Arab slave trader named Zubair had defeated and killed the native sultan and collected a large private army. However. when he went to Cairo, expecting to be made a sultan himself, he found that the Khedive Ismail was nervous of his power and instead detained him and sent him to serve with the Turkish armies fighting Russia.

In the meantime Zubair had left his son Suleiman in charge of his armies with which he continued to make slave raids. On 31st August 1877 Gordon learned that Suleiman had advanced on Dara with a large force of armed slaves, with the intention of taking the weak Egyptian garrison there. He set out on his racing camel with a few hundred men to the rescue and there followed one of the best known incidents in Gordon's remarkable career.

At dawn on the 2nd September 1877, he put on his magnificent marshal's gold braided uniform (my gold armour), mounted a horse and 'with an escort of my robbers of Bashi Bazouks, rode out to the camp of the other robbers 3 miles off. I was met by the son of Zubair, a nice looking lad of 22 years and rode through the robber bands, there were about 3,000 of them, boys and men. I rode to the tent in the camp, the whole of these chiefs were dumbfounded at my coming among them; after a glass of water, I went back, telling the son of Zubair to come with his family to my Divan".

It would have been the easiest thing in the world for the white-robed warriors to have speared him to death - but Gordon not only showed no fear but also a good understanding of the Arab mentality.

The next day Suleiman turned up at Dara with his advisers. They accepted Gordon's coffee "and sitting there in a circle I gave them, in choice Arabic, my ideas; that they meditated revolt, that I knew it, and that they should now hear my ultimatum, viz, that I would disarm them and break them up. They listened in silence, and then went off to consider what I have said." Suleiman sent a letter of submission and after some days returned to his base at Shaka where Gordon accepted his submission and the dispersal of his army.

Gordon's great aim was the abolition of the slave trade and on his journey from Abyssinia to Khartoum earlier in the year he had devised a scheme towards this end. He sent the details to Hussey Vivian, the British Consul-General in Cairo and these became the basis of the Anglo-Egyptian Convention 'for the suppression of the Slave Trade' signed in August 1877: All masters must register their slaves, including runaways, before 1st January 1878, when registration would stop: no man or woman enslaved after that date would be the legal property of the master and could therefore run with impunity. Sales between masters would continue to be legal but the market for new slaves would decline since no sale would have the force of law. By the Convention slavery would be abolished in 1889.

Under Gordon's rule the Sudan was being better governed than it had ever been, but there were always a fresh set of problems. He was no figurehead governor-general ruling from his Palace in Khartoum and whenever a crisis occurred in the tribal lands he would immediately undertake another of his formidable camel journeys to the scene of disturbance.

Meanwhile Lieutenant Brocklehurst, having been prevented from serving under Gordon, had slipped comfortably back into the fashionable London scene, which Gordon so despised, and soon had matters other than the Sudan on his mind.

CHAPTER FOUR

During the London season Hyde Park was then the centre for courtship and display among fashionable society. To be seen driving in an open carriage through the park, or riding together in Rotten Row (so-called from it's original name of Route du Roi -the King's Road) was considered to be a declaration of intent, or at least of interest. Soon the gossips were observing that a young officer in the Blues was frequently to be seen riding out with Miss Louisa Parsons, the granddaughter of Lord Feversham and one of the Row's 'fairest and best known flowers'.

That Autumn of 1877 Lieutenant John Fielden Brocklehurst and Miss Louisa Alice Parsons announced their engagement. "Letter from Johnny - short and sweet - announcing his engagement to a Miss Parsons, living near Windsor", his aunt Emma Dent recorded."Anything less interesting than his note not to be imagined", she complained.

"And so the first Mrs Brocklehurst of a new generation is to be introduced among us. Further information comes that her father was son to Lord Moss of telescopic celebrity - the Hon Lawrence Parsons- her mother a daughter of Lord Feversham - that she is pretty and gentle and quiet, not at all fast and it is thought will make Johnny a very good wife."

By December we learn that Louie (as Louisa was known) is to have £200 a year for allowance and Papa P talks of settling seventeen or eighteen thousand on her at his death. In the meantime she and Johnny were staying at Badminton with the Duke and Duchess of Beaufort, who were going to give the couple spoons and forks as a wedding present.

Louie was also being well received by the Brocklehurst family in Macclesfield. Johnny's Uncle William wrote enthusiastically to Emma Dent, "everyone describes the bride elect as very ladylike - rather petite, rather delicate - very nice - just the sort to capture a lad like Johnny and hold him in silken chains. She seems to have taken kindly to her new relations and quite inclined to accept a place amongst us.

They have rented a house at Windsor, and propose to reside there for the next two years and the soldier will continue in the Army during that time. I think and hope he will remain till he gets his troop - the young lady will have a tidy fortune of her own which she will get at the death of her father, who is 71."

Gordon was the first person Brocklehurst wanted to tell about his impending marriage, but the two letters he had written to him - in October and December 1877 did not reach Gordon until the 5th January 1878 where he was staying "in the windy house at Massowah". His reply was predictable. "I congratulate you sincerely on your marriage, I am truly glad of it, for it will settle you and prevent you going on wild expeditions", he wrote. "I often think of you, I may say daily.

I hope you will have a very happy life and everything to comfort you and your future wife, oblige me and do not be angry with me in saying it, have family prayers from the very beginning of your new life. Honour Him and He will tenfold honour you."

Gordon's advice on marriage had already been given to other of his young bachelor friends, like Charles Watson - "Till a man is married he is a selfish fellow, however he may wish not to be so. Remember that by marrying you are no longer free for quixotic expeditions; you are bound to consider your better half; nothing is more selfish than a married man seeking adventures which his wife *cannot partake in*". He did not realise then that he would put Brocklehurst in just such a dilemma when six years later he asked him to go with him on his last fatal mission to Khartoum.

When asked once why he had never married Gordon had replied that he had never met a woman who "for my sake, and perhaps at a moment's notice would be prepared to sacrifice the comforts of home, and the sweet society of loved ones, and accompany me whithersoever the demand of duty might lead - accompany me to the ends of the earth perhaps; would stand by me in times of danger and difficulty, and sustain me in times of hardship and perplexity".

Johnny Brocklehurst believed that he had found such a woman in Louie and she was to prove later that when possible she was prepared to 'pack and follow' her man.

Their marriage was celebrated in style at St Peter's Eaton Square in London on the 25th February 1878. The bride wore a 'white Sicilienne Princesse dress, trimmed with white satin and Brussels lace' with a wreath of natural orange blossoms in her hair fastened by diamond stars and a necklace and bracelets of diamonds and pearls. As befitted a winter wedding the seven bridesmaids wore ruby velvet dresses - also *a la princesse* - with collars of antique Irish point, and sported matching ruby velvet hats with ostrich feathers. They included the bride's younger sister, Florence Parsons and the bridegroom's sister Annie

Brocklehurst. The ceremony was performed by the Hon. and Rev. Randal Parsons, the bride's cousin and Lord Arthur Somerset acted as best man.

The guest list was as glittering as the bride's jewellery, studded with viscounts, countesses, lords and ladies and one duchess. with the Brocklehurst family coming well down the 'pecking order'. The reception was held at the Parsons house in Eaton Square and 'the bridal presents were numerous' according to a newspaper report 'and some of costly character.'

Johnny wrote to Aunt Emma from Cannes, where they were on honeymoon, to thank her for her £100 wedding present with which to buy a piano and for the two small portraits she gave him of his father and grandfather painted by the Worcester painter Josiah Rushton. On their return she learned that he had bought a house called 'The Willows' near Windsor. "It will be very pleasant for Louie as the Parsons live only a few miles away at Winkfield Place", Emma noted. "However, we hear it is fearfully damp and in the winter the garden is under water from the Thames".

At the start of the London season Louie was 'named' in the Court Journal as a newly married member of society 'June 1878 In the Queen's Drawing Room at Buckingham Palace on Tuesday. Mrs J F Brocklehurst was presented on her marriage by her mother, the Hon Mrs Parsons'. The Brocklehursts began to fear that the young couple were becoming altogether too grand for them.

Emma and John Dent were concerned the following autumn when "Johnny and his wife, staying at the Duke of Beaufort's write to offer themselves for a week's hunting at Sudeley - to bring six horses - which would involve we suppose three or four grooms besides his valet and her maid", Emma wrote in her diary. "John not well enough to be at home - this proposition gave him something of an alarm - and we were obliged to decline them. We think also that their servants coming from such an establishment as the Duke's would have been very discontented with the simple arrangements and frugal fare of our little menage".

The young couple wrote to her later from their home, 'The Willows' with the news that their field had become a lake owing to the River Thames being so high and that there were 20 swans swimming about on it.

Meanwhile in the Sudan events were not going well for Gordon. First he had been summoned to Cairo to help set up a board of inquiry to deal with the £80 million debt Egypt now owed to its European creditors, including the English and French governments. This led to his first meeting with the newly-appointed British Commissioner in Egypt - Captain Evelyn Baring. He disliked him on first sight. Baring was a typical member of the establishment. "He has a pretentious, grand, patronising way about him", Gordon noted. "When oil mixes with water we will mix together".

Finance had never been one of Gordon's major concerns. He had already offered a cut in salary and was paying his own expenses when on tour, including buying 72 camels for himself and his entourage. But when he wrote a paper for the inquiry suggesting that the interest on the creditors' bonds should be suspended for a year and the money used to pay civil and military salaries, which were well in arrears, he was overruled. And when it became evident that the inquiry was loaded in favour of the international creditors, he resigned and returned to Khartoum.

By the summer of 1879 all his good work in the Sudan was beginning to unravel. Ismail, the man who had given him the

Sudan was forced to abdicate in favour of his son Tewfik, and Zubair's son Suleiman had been killed by Gessi, an old colleague of Gordon's, while acting as governor of Bahr-el-Ghazal in a war against the slave traders. Gordon did not like Tewfik, nor the ruling clique of Egyptian pashas in Cairo.

In July 1879 he determined to resign as Governor-General of the Sudan, but before doing so he was persuaded by Tewfik to undertake another of his prodigious rides into Abyssinia - "thirty-eight weary days riding a mule through interminable mountains" - in an attempt to obtain a final peace settlement between Egypt and King John. The Abyssinians arrested him and turned him out and he finally struggled back to Cairo to find that the Egyptian governors who he had dismissed and the British officials who considered him too headstrong and erratic had united to destroy him. He was now sick and desperately tired and was relieved when Tewfik accepted his resignation and he was free to leave Egypt.

In the meanwhile his belief that Johnny Brocklehurst's marriage would prevent him from undertaking any more 'wild expeditions' was proved wrong when in August 1879 Johnny and Louie set off to spend his generous four months leave from the Army in Canada and the United States - "to live in tents and on what they shoot. No maid, and Louie has taken a gun wherewith to furnish her own larder!"

By September Johnny was writing enthusiastically to his aunt Emma Dent as she recorded in her diary: "They've got twelve horses, a wagon, a black cook and a French maid (the latter Sir Bache Cunard got for them) and she is a treasure, can wash, cook and shoot. They had a very tiring journey there, but Louie is beginning to take very kindly to camp life and no longer minds strange animals walking over her at night, or imagines every loose horse a scalping Indian. She has also become a dead shot and there is plenty for her to shoot, namely jack rabbits, confiding sage hens and blue grouse, all excellent eating. Their party so far have been too fond of letting their guns off at antelope and blacktail, both excellent in their way, but they've driven the elk away, so on Tuesday they start on a 200 mile march north to the big Horn Mountain where the buffalo still are. Buffalo were very plentiful where they were a short time ago, but they are driving them north every day and very shortly both they and the Indians will be a thing of the past.

Johnny has got (himself) two great monster bull elk, besides other deer, and wounded a bear the other night - the bear was eating one of the elk and he only got a galloping shot at him, which however knocked him down and enabled Johnny to run (very much blown) within 50 yards of him, until the bear scrambled into some timber and was lost. All the shooting is done at sunrise and sunset and precious cold it is sometimes. There is generally ice a quarter of an inch thick on the water in the morning. The price of a horse 15 hands is £10 to £15. The horses are loose at night but do not stray much. Their next address is at E Frewen Esq. Powder River, Fort F Mirman, Wyoming, United States."

The Frewen brothers had recently moved to the United States to start cattle raising and had set up their 76 Ranch along the banks of the North Powder River and the Crazy Women - practically on the site of General Custer's last stand and 300 miles from the nearest railway at Little Rock.

Hugh Lowther, the Earl of Lonsdale and his wife Grace were among several well-known English aristocrats who had gathered at the 76 Ranch for the shooting. According to Grace Lowther she and Mrs Brocklehurst were the only women in the original party - "but Mrs Brocklehurst proved an early casualty. Finding that the ground was unsuitable for carriages she and her husband returned to Britain".

This was obviously not so, because a month later Johnny and Louie sent Emma Dent a letter from a camp 300 miles from Rock Creek where they had left the railway. Part of the way they had ridden, part trundled in government ambulances - escorted by soldiers who cause them much amusement. Johnny had shot two of the nine bears killed by their party. Louie had seen Johnny kill a buffalo and had assisted in skinning and amputating the head, which was too heavy to put on their pony, and still worse had detained them so that they could not find the rest of the party which had moved camp in their absence. Luckily they knew the way back to their old camp site where two of the hunters were left to finish some skinning and spent the night there before rejoining their party next day.

Grace Lowther meanwhile had mistakenly set fire to the prairie destroying one of their waggons containing Hugh Lowther's outfit and a supply of valuable shoes. The rest of the party had their baggage on mules, so escaped any damage, although according to Grace the fire continued to burn for two weeks.

In his letter Johnny said that the last battle fought with the Indians had been 18 months before and five miles from their last camp. "They got the worst of it - poor things - now only friendly tribes are left - we expect a visit from the Rappaloes - but they are also friendly. Our party now consists of 10 men (including hunters), three women, 19 horses, three mules, two cows, two calves, three dogs and a donkey! We have three more weeks of tent life - then back to Rock Creek and so to San Francisco - and sail from New York on the 19th November."

At the beginning of November they were in Florida and off up the Sewanee River after alligator and wild turkeys, but they succeeded in getting back to Liverpool on the due day and Brocklehurst was back on Army duty again on the 1st December.

It had been a "most prosperous and adventurous tour in the Rocky Mountains and he had killed nine bears out of the 21 shot." Louie had proved herself to be a brave and resourceful companion not a 'fragile flower' and they looked forward to more big-game adventures together, little realising that Johnny would soon be on active service.

CHAPTER FIVE

When Johnny Brocklehurst was commissioned in the Royal Horse Guards in 1874 the Household Cavalry was considered , in Army terms, to be handsome but useless. The regiment's proud record of gallantry at Waterloo and previously in the Peninsular War, when they were specially commended by the Duke of Wellington, had been obscured by seventy years absence from the Fighting Army, and they were now best known as the 'ornamental soldiers' who took part in Court and State functions.

Even in this role they were sometimes ridiculed - "The Blues were unavoidably prevented from attending morning service the other Sunday at Windsor, owing to a shower of rain", mocked *The World*. "I understand that HRH the Duke of Cambridge has ordered umbrellas for the crack corps and that until Sangster has executed this order the gallant fellows will pretermit their devotions. The weather is really so uncertain that it is felt too risky to send them to church without this insurance against the cold. It might drizzle, you see, after the function was over, and the notion of a 'Blue' being rained upon is quite appalling".

Fortunately for the Brigade, and particularly for Brocklehurst, they were able to shed their 'ornamental' image and join the first cavalry force since Waterloo, to fight in the Egyptian War of 1882 .Although Gladstone had been anxious not to get involved in Egypt, the country had become more important to Britain since the opening of the Suez Canal and Disraeli's purchase of Suez Canal shares had led to joint responsibility for the territory with France.

The fighting started when a nationalistic revolt in Egypt against the foreigners, led by one of the Army commanders, Colonel Arabi resulted in riots in Alexandria in which 50 Europeans were killed. When Arabi started to mount guns in the port, which were a threat to all the ships in the harbour ,and ignored the British ultimatum to stop, the Mediterranean Fleet bombarded Alexandria, while the French ,who had more pressing problems in Europe at the time, sailed back home.

Following the British bombardment Arabi retreated with his army towards Cairo, threatening to blow up the Suez Canal and cancel Egypt's foreign debt. This was a twist too much in the lion's tail and Gladstone ordered a British Army unit headed by Sir Garnet Wolseley to take Cairo, smash the Egyptian Army and restore good government.

Great was the rejoicing in the barracks at Knightsbridge, Regents Park and Windsor when the men of the Household Cavalry heard that Wolseley's Army would include a considerable force of cavalry. A composite regiment, made up of a squadron each from the 1st and 2nd Life Guards and the Royal Horse Guards was ordered.

As we would expect Brocklehurst, who had been promoted to Captain in 1881,was among the first officers of the Brigade to volunteer and was selected to accompany Colonel Milne-Home, his own immediate chief, to Egypt in command of a troop of the composite regiment.

The force set sail from England on the 1st August and on the 11th Johnny wrote to his brother, Harry: "Just a line to say we are getting on tiptop and everything has got shipshape. The Bosses being most agreeable cocks. We get to Malta tomorrow morning and are getting very much excited as to what the news may be. Very martial being the talk which comes, I suppose, from sleeping in a cabin full of swords and pistols. With one or two exceptions the horses are doing very well. Rostron gets plenty of exercise, being sent for at all hours by nervous owners. McGhur [his horse] has got pleurisy from overeating himself. It seems for the first week his next door neighbours lost their appetites, while he very much retained his, so he nearly burst. My charges are some on deck, some below, some at one end and some at the other, so stables, of which we have four hours a day, is a lively time for me."

Once landed in Egypt Wolseley had decided to concentrate his force on Ismalia and particularly to protect his water supply by taking the Lock at Kassassin on the fresh water canal which connected the Nile at Cairo with the Suez Canal at Ismalia. On the 3rd September Brocklehurst and the cavalry were camped between Mahsameh Camp and Kassassin,. "We had very rough work at first", he wrote to his Aunt Marianne, "very short of food for men and horses; none at all for 48 hours. When we took Mahsameh Camp Oh such loot, but I was too busy to look after it, and afterwards too dead beat. I'd have given the Koh-i-noor for a water melon.

"Our Moonlight Charge at Kassassin frightened the Egyptians and gave us some rest; it was all by moonlight and was a weird and ghastly proceeding. We came on some infantry, their left wing, rather unexpectedly, but we promptly charged them. For the first few minutes it looked as if they meant to shoot us down; and then it was our men's turn to butcher them. It was a strong force and I cannot think why they did not shoot us all. I suppose our men cheering made them fire wild".

An official description of the charge recorded that General Graham was in touch with the enemy at Kassassin on August 28th when the cavalry force, under General Drury Lowe, advancing in obedience to a message from Graham, found itself suddenly exposed to a combined artillery and infantry fire. The Household Cavalry, led by Colonel Ewart, charged and absolutely annihilated the force which they struck upon, but did not reach the Egyptian artillery, owing to the darkness and the absence of any "points" upon which to move in the open desert. Brocklehurst, who was in the forefront of the charge, sustained a damaged knee which fortunately was not serious enough to keep him out of the main battle..

"We did form in Battle Array in your dear old Desert (you shall have my share of it)", he wrote to Aunt Marianne. Wolseley had resolved on a direct attack on the formidable entrenchments of the Egyptian army at Tel-el-Khebir. The attack to be delivered at dawn on September 13th, after a night march from Kassassin.

The night was a dark one, and there was difficulty in finding the directing posts which had been set up by the Royal Engineers as guides for the earlier part of the march. By 11 pm the army (17,000 men with 67 guns) was in battle order and at 1.30 am moved westwards over the silent desert. Fixing bayonets as they advanced, the Highlanders were within 150 yards of the enemy's pickets when they were discovered. A few shots were fired by the Egyptian sentries; then their bugles sounded and directly the whole front of the parapet was lit up for a mile or so by the flash of rifles. The long night's silence was at length broken, first by our buglers sounding the advance, then by a ringing cheer as the other bugles repeated and the Highlanders rushed in two long waves upon the rampart.

Meanwhile the cavalry, 3000 sabres, had been sent by night round the right flank. "We formed up Regsm posted and each man slept with his horse in line of battle", reported Brocklehurst, "(This means tying your bridle round your wrist, lying flat on your back in the sand, with all your arms on, and going to sleep, that is if the nag permits).McGhur was much too astonished at the whole affair to admit of my sleeping; the poor old fellow kept sniffing and snorting in my face, as if wanting to know what it all meant. That night was an experience for us both. I wish you could have seen that waiting for the first gun to proclaim the attack on the works, when off we went as hard as we could go, to cut the railway and do what damage we could."

By 6 am the battle was over. Arabi was huddled up in a railway carriage trying to make his escape and the cavalry had started on a 65 mile dash to Cairo with instructions to "spare neither man nor horse if Cairo could be saved from destruction". Brocklehurst described it as "a hard march, 60 hours without the saddles off and we did not lose a horse. On one occasion after snatching a couple of hours rest on the sand it was startling to find I had been lying on a scorpion, and I was not sorry to see in the distance our old friends the Pyramids, for then I knew we were nearing Cairo and ending our forced march".

At 10 pm on the night of September 14th Captain Watson with 150 men rode into the Cairo citadel and the garrison of 5,000 men marched out. Arabi was a prisoner and Cairo surrendered to the cavalry.

After a successful campaign of only three short weeks Britain now controlled Egypt, but while the enemy had been routed, the conditions for the fighting men were very bad. "It is very hot and stuffy here now, and the men are going sick very fast", wrote Johnny from Cairo to Aunt Marianne. "You see the Nile is out and going down, leaving a lot of black mud for the sun to slime upon, and breed fever. It's a bad thing for a man to go sick as there is, and has been, no sort of hospital care. I believe sick men are being starved to death thro' the laziness of the doctors. This department has been inhumanly disgraceful, as I know from some of my own men, and the transport is not much better".

Florence Nightingale reading reports from Cairo said, "It is the Crimea over again". Supplies were not available to the troops in the right place. The hospital equipment was insufficient and unsuitable for the climate. Supplies of drugs, dressings and instruments ran out and cooking arrangements broke down. She sent a party of 24 nurses out to Cairo but the proportion of sick men was unduly high and only the small number of troops and the short duration of the campaign prevented disaster.

Despite this Wolseley himself looked upon the campaign as the best-managed exercise in British military history at the time and the victory earned him a peerage. For Johnny Brocklehurst it proved to be an important opportunity to come to the notice of the great soldier, who was already a byword in the Army - "All Sir Garnet" being the current term for "all present and correct"- as well as being immortalised by Gilbert as the Modern Major-General in the *"Pirates of Penzance"*.

Queen Victoria personally reviewed the victorious troops on their return and Johnny sent his 'spoils of war' to Aunt Nem -

Emma Dent of Sudeley Castle - to add to the small museum she was creating in the Castle. "I send you a Remington rifle and bayonet, a trumpet and knapsack found in the Egyptian Camp at Mahsameh, which was taken by the Household Cavalry, 7th Dragoon Guard and two Batteries of Horse Artillery on August 25. There are also two native fans and a fly flipper. The knapsack wants the board arranging to make him nice and square.

The Campaign is over and a good job too. Dust, sun, flies and putrid water being some of the chief items and I was lame half the time from a crack I got on my knee in our moonlight charge. That was a curious scene, some shells had begun bursting among us, we could not tell from where, when suddenly the ridge of desert in front of us lit up like a great cracker and there was a perfect storm of bullets - rather high luckily. Front line charge, then such a spatter, dust, stones and bullets a dirty job it was all by the light of the moon."

By the time Brocklehurst had returned from Egypt Gordon was at his sister Augusta's house at Rockstone Place in Southampton after restlessly working round the world since his resignation from the Sudan in 1879. He was pleased to hear of Brocklehurst's exploits in the Egyptian War - "RB Brett says you are a splendid fellow, which I know", he wrote. "I am sorry for the Egyptians. Do you know that Arabi came off and met you and me at Massawah in 1877? He was a smart fellow then. Osman Rifki Pasha was also in the Boat which came off, the same man who was put in prison by Arabi afterwards."

Earlier he had written to Brocklehurst from Port Louis where he enjoyed a brief interlude as Governor of Mauritius and became enthused with the idea that the Seychelles were the site of the Garden of Eden. "The trees are the Bread Fruit and the so-called Coco-de-mer, which is only found at Praslin, an isle near the Seychelles - you will laugh and want to see the Forbidden tree, well I cannot describe it, but you would laugh if you saw it - though the trouble it caused us is no laughing matter", he wrote.

In April 1882 Gordon had been promoted to Major-General and decided to take a year's leave from the Army studying the Bible in Palestine and the Holy Land. "You must try and come out" he told Brocklehurst. "You are never forgotten, every morning I come and see you in spirit" This I think referred to his remembering Brocklehurst in his prayers. Wolseley's biographers say that Gordon told Wolseley that two of the men he prayed for daily were Wolseley himself - his old comrade of the trenches before Sebastopol - and the young Brocklehurst. As always he included in his letters good wishes to Louie and to the MB's who he had jokingly christened "the Foreign Office".

While Gordon was pursuing his Biblical studies in the Holy Land, which resulted in him proposing alternative sites for Calvary and the Garden Tomb, and at the very time that the victorious army was dispersed after delivering Egypt into British hands came a note of alarm from Khartoum, from the Governor-General of the Sudan, Abdul Kader Pasha, who telegraphed that the troops he had sent against the Mahdi had been destroyed.

Who was the Mahdi? There are confused accounts of his origins but Muhammad Ahmad Abdallah, was said to have been the son of a carpenter and a native of Dongola. He was deeply religious and when he became adult went to live on the Island of Abba on the White Nile where, surrounded by several devoted disciples, he hollowed out a cave in the mudbank and lived there in seclusion, fasting often for days. A quarrel with his old preceptor Muhammad Sheraf, is supposed to have led to his advancement as "a holy man" and to his declaration that he was the Mahdi el Muntassah, the expected guide and messenger of god who Muhammad had predicted would one day appear and restore the true faith of Islam. With the aim of wresting the Sudan from Egypt he raised a cry for a Jihad - a Holy War. The flame of active rebellion was kindled and was soon burning throughout the length and breadth of the country.

In August 1882 the Mahdi laid siege to El Obeid - a town of some10,000 people protected by a strong Egyptian garrison. When the city fell after a six months siege he acquired for the first time a large store of arms and money and the spears and shields which, with a few ancient muskets had been his only weapons, were replaced with modern rifles and ammunition. He now commanded an awesome killing machine and embarked on a course of remorseless slaughter as religious fanaticism swept through the Sudan.

Worse was to follow. As the British Government turned its back on the Sudan, with Gladstone determined to have no further involvement in Africa, Egypt had to raise its own force against the Mahdi. The command was given to William Hicks of the Bombay Army who set out in September 1883 with some 7,000 infantry, 1,000 cavalry and more than 5,000 camels which were needed to carry desert supplies and equipment including machine guns and ammunition. Led by supposedly friendly guides they marched westwards across the desert until on the 5th November exhausted by thirst they had halted in the depths of a dry forest when they were ambushed by 50,000 Arab warriors. The Egyptian troops, many of whom were peasant conscripts who had been dragged in chains from their homes to fight, threw down their weapons and only a few hundred of the 10,000 man force survived the vicious attack. Hicks and his European officers were among the dead - their bodies left to rot in the sand, except for Hicks' head which was cut off and sent in a sack to the Mahdi.

When news of the Hicks disaster reached England a Colonel in the Royal Engineers, living at Folkestone, remembered 20 years earlier seeing another fanatical horde in China collapse before the skill and genius of a young British officer. Colonel Edwards wrote to the inspector general of fortifications, General Sir Andrew Clarke RE - "There is one man who is competent to deal with this question - Charlie Gordon". This letter found its way to Granville, the Foreign Secretary and thus into the highest councils of the land.

CHAPTER SIX

Apparently unperturbed by the situation in the Sudan Gordon had made up his mind to accept the offer which King Leopold of the Belgians had been dangling over him for some time, to join with Henry Morton Stanley in opening up the recently discovered Congo. On his journey back from Palestine he disembarked at Genoa and went overland to Brussels where Brocklehurst met him and they were received by King Leopold on the 2nd January.

What is now known to have been a greedy exploitation of the Congo by Leopold during the African 'land grab' was presented as a much more philanthropic venture to Gordon and Brocklehurst., who described it in a letter to Aunt Marianne.

"Some ten years ago or more Leopold lost his son, a boy of 12 years of age, and he determined to execute some great scheme for the good of the World 'In Memoriam', and settled on the opening up of the Congo at his own expense for the good of everyone. Stanley is now the man who is carrying the work on, making stations up the river. (There are stations now two thousand miles up, and the King, has already spent £500,000 and over, on it), but Gordon is the man he wants and Gordon has promised to go, but his ideas are not so much for commerce as for the suppression of the Slave Trade. You will see that the Head waters of the Congo are close to his old province of "the Lakes" ....Our friend Gordon will teach the slaves or niggers to protect themselves, and so goodbye to Slavery.

"I had a long private interview with King Leopold about it when I was in Brussels with Gordon and he was most kind and explained it all to me", Brocklehurst wrote.

The King badly needed Gordon to give respectability to the venture and Gordon himself was enthused by the prospect, although he realised that going to the Congo would probably mean he would have to resign his commission in the British Army. He was relieved when King Leopold promised to compensate him for the probable loss of his Army pension.

However, others were not so enthusiastic, particularly his old Army friend Wolseley. In a letter to Gordon in Brussels he said "You have had enough of liver-grilling climates, and the world does not seem bounded with the clear horizon that would warrant - if I may venture to say so to an old friend - our very best man burying himself amongst niggers on the Equator. Of course, if you will go there, all will go right for King Leopold, and I am very anxious his project should succeed, but I think he might attain his end without taking our best man from the English Army". He went on to promise to help Gordon to retain his commission and said he would like to talk to him about the Sudan.

He was not alone. There was a growing groundswell of opinion in Britain demanding action of some kind in the Sudan, following Hicks defeat. At the forefront was the pioneering journalist W T Stead.

William Thomas Stead was only twenty-two when he became editor of the *Northern Echo*, a daily paper published in Darlington, where he first began to be noticed for his articles on the Bulgarian Atrocities in 1876. By 1883 he was in London editing the *Pall Mall Gazette*, a ' tuppeny' evening paper which was originally printed in a warehouse at the river end of the old Adelphi arches, close to a 'Half-penny Boat Pier from where the porters carried fruit and vegetable to Covent Garden Market'. Later, housed in Northumberland Avenue, it was to become a vigorous voice of the emerging 'new journalism' - strident, courageous and influential.

In that momentous January of 1884 it was the first newspaper to get the news of Gordon's Congo appointment and Stead published a paragraph lamenting "when so much was urgently needing to be done in Egypt the services of the ablest leader of irregular forces England had produced should be lost to the country".

Gordon had agreed with King Leopold to leave for the Congo early in February, after first returning to England to resign his commission, and he and Brocklehurst left the Belle Vue Hotel in Brussels on the 8th January.

"The Establishment turned out to see the great General go", Brocklehurst wrote to Aunt Marianne. "First came the Proprietor, a great swell, with whom Gordon shook hands, much to his delight. Next came the Head Waiter, a great swell, whom I also shook by the hand to the disgust of the Proprietor. Then came the Boots, not at all a swell, whom Gordon shook warmly by the hand. I wish you could have seen No.1's face!"

They arrived back in England that evening only to find at Gordon's sister Augusta's house at Rockstone Place in

Southampton a telegram from Stead asking for permission to visit him and discuss the Sudan problem. Gordon wired back that his views were of insufficient importance to justify a journey from London - but Stead persisted. He was to become the first 'door-stepping' interviewer.

"Today came a Mr Stead and invaded me" Gordon wrote to Sir Samuel Baker after the interview, and much has been made of the fact that Gordon himself answered the door to Stead.

Stead's biographer, Frederic Whyte, painted a vivid picture of the sitting-room at Rockstone Place as its three occupants sat drinking tea -" Gordon, Stead and Gordon's intimate friend - from this date onwards one of Stead's closest allies - Captain Brocklehurst.

Stead sat on a couch covered with leopard skin - a rapt listener, his strange blue eyes fixed on Gordon's own. Brocklehurst, handsome, refined-looking, keeping almost complete silence one imagines - full of admiration for Gordon, interested and puzzled by, but surprisingly taken with, this impetuous, exuberant newspaper man, not quite like anybody he had seen before. Gordon himself slightly built, somewhat below the average height. General Gordon's most remarkable characteristic at first sight is childlike simplicity of speech and manners. Notwithstanding 50 years, his face is almost boyish in its youthfulness, his step is as light and his movements as lithe as the leopard".

Gordon had spread a map of the Congo on the floor and at first would talk of nothing else. He planned to join with Emin in Equatoria - to advance and conquer, not merely to rescue and retire.Stead asked how he thought he would get on with Stanley, to which Gordon characteristically replied "If it is God's will it will be done. We will go there".

His aim was to strike north from the Congo towards the Mohammedan States so as to narrow the area of No Man's Land where the slave traders ply their calling. "Here I believe the great work will be accomplished", he said. The Arabs would not come 10 degrees below the equator because their camels would not live.

This was all very well but Stead was impatient to hear his views on the Sudan. Was Egypt to be forced by England to abandon the provinces of Lower Egypt? What should be done about saving the garrisons in Khartoum, Darfur, Bahr-el-Ghazal and Gondoroko?

Gordon said the provinces of Darfur and Kordofan would have to be abandoned but the defence of Khartoum was essential. A Governor General should be appointed with full powers and, with his usual modesty he suggested that Sir Samuel Baker rather than he should take on the task. He mistakenly refused to believe that the Mahdi was a dangerous religious leader. All the Sudanese were potential Mahdis, just as all the Egyptians were potential Arabis. What they needed was good government. They were 'a very nice people' he knew them well and loved them much. They deserved the sincere sympathy and compassion of all civilised men. The real danger was the effect on other Mahommedans of the Mahdi's successes which were already causing ferment in Syria and Arabia. The conflict between Christianity and Islam could spread across the Middle East.

The two hour long interview ended with Gordon saying he did not want to press his opinions. Brocklehurst agreed to go back to London with Stead and checked the record of the interview at the *Pall Mall Gazette* office the following morning - Stead having dictated it to his secretary during the night. It was amazingly accurate - "only one name wrong" Brocklehurst recalled some years later in a letter to Stead's daughter, Estelle. "A truly marvellous effort for Gordon talked very fast and your father did not take a note."

The interview was published in the paper that evening under the heading 'Chinese Gordon on the Soudan" with a leading article by Stead saying "Why not send Chinese Gordon to Khartoum with full powers to assume absolute control of the territory, to treat with the Mahdi, to relieve the garrisons and to do what can be done to save what can be saved from the wreck of the Soudan?"

Meanwhile Gordon went to see Samuel Baker, who he was still insisting should command the action. Baker thought otherwise. He urged Gordon to forget about the Congo and return to the Sudan and when Gordon wrote him a letter setting out his views Baker passed it to *The Times* which published it on the 14th January. By this time most of the London papers had jumped on Stead's bandwagon and the public were also in full cry for Gordon.to be sent to the Sudan.

The following day he met Wolseley at the War Office. The latter had been working with Lord Hartington, the Minister of War and Lord Granville the Foreign Secretary to persuade Gladstone that intervention was needed in the Sudan and Gordon who knew the Sudan intimately was the obvious choice. Beside Gladstone's indecision the only other problem was Sir Evelyn Baring, who was the British Agent and Consul General in Cairo. Baring and Gordon were old antagonists from Gordon's previous time in the Sudan, and Baring had declared Gordon 'quite unfit'.

When Wolseley and Gordon met on the 15th January Wolseley told Gordon that he would be allowed to serve in the

Congo without resigning his commission, but in the meantime there were more pressing tasks to be done for his own country. He appealed to Gordon's patriotism and asked whether he would be prepared to go to Suakin and enquire into the condition of affairs in the Sudan. Gordon agreed, but insisted that if he was going to break his agreement with King Leopold he should do so in person. He spent a day saying goodbye to old friends, including Baroness Burdett-Coutts who gave him her lettercase as a keepsake, before he and Brocklehurst left for Brussels on the overnight train.

However, he never even had time to have an audience with the King because they reached the Hotel Belle Vue to find a telegram from Wolseley sent at noon on the 17th January.

"Come here at once can you start this evening so as to be with me early tomorrow telegraph at once saying hour tomorrow I may expect you".

Gordon and Brocklehurst recrossed the Channel overnight and arrived in London early in the morning of the 18th January.

Granville had wired Baring for the third time about sending Gordon to the Sudan and Baring had finally given in. He later said he never ceased to regret that he had consented , and had yielded only because everyone was against him. He insisted that Gordon was to take orders from him in Cairo and was to make it clear that he understood that his duties were to report on the Sudan and get the garrison out if he could, but that was all.

At noon on the 18th Gordon attended a meeting of those members of the Cabinet who were in London - Parliament was still in recess and Gladstone was at his country house near Chester -. Wolseley had told Gordon that the Government was determined to evacuate the Sudan and when he was asked if he was prepared to go and do it, Gordon agreed.

He sent this account of the meeting to his sister Augusta: "At noon he, Wolseley, came to me and took me to the Ministers. He went in and talked to the Ministers and came back and said 'Her Majesty's Government want you to understand this. The Government are determined to evacuate the Sudan for they will not guarantee future government. You will go and do it? I said 'yes'. He said 'Go in'. I went in and saw them and they said did Wolseley tell you our ideas? I said 'yes. He said you will not guarantee future government of the Sudan and you wish me to go and evacuate it?' They said 'yes' and it was over...."

With what dispatch were decisions made and actions taken in those days. There was no doubt that Gordon was going on a difficult and dangerous mission to the Sudan and yet he was barely given time to pack. By 8 pm the same evening he was at Charing Cross station where Wolseley, Granville and the Duke of Cambridge had come to see him off. At the last minute they discovered that Gordon, as usual had only a few shillings in his pocket and Wolseley pressed on him his own spare cash as well as his gold watch and chain.

Brocklehurst was not there. Gordon had dined with him in the Blues mess that evening, but the train left without him. "Gordon asked me to go with him and I said no, and feel pretty low" he said in a letter to Aunt Marianne..

"He started last night as British Commissioner, which I suppose means a Commission to get a lot of old women called the British Government out of a mess He will go straight to Khartoum with instruction to form a native Government there and then sever its connection with Egypt. He intends to go to Khartoum via Suakim by making Sheikh Moussa (who holds the Berber, Suakim road to Khartoum) escort him. It seems that in 1878 he spared the lives of three of Sheikh Moussa's sons, so he is beholden to him.

"Now with respect to giving up Khartoum you will remember that the Nilometer is there, which gives lower Egypt 21 days notice as to what to expect in the way of a flood and thereby regulates the corvee, so for no other reason ordinary mortals would say it is impossible to abandon it - but Gordon means to follow instructions, as he has pledged himself, namely, as he calls it, cut the dog's tail off, but I hope, and have reason to think, that when Gordon is once there the Government will do as he tells them if he finds the dog's tail wont come off.

Arrived at Khartoum, he will summon the Tribes, remind them he is their friend, always has been and that now he has come to give them their freedom from Egyptian mis-rule, and will there and then appoint them his escort and protectors." Gordon says this insurrection is all his doing, as he taught the people of the Soudan a better form of Government, and when he left they refused to go back to the old "Bashi Bazook" system which Tewfik tried to force on them. "I laid the egg which the Mahdi has hatched", he claimed.

"In the meantime I go back to Oakham tomorrow, where Louie is anxiously waiting." Brocklehurst wrote. "Do you think I did right not to go?"

His place with Gordon was filled at the last minute by one of Wolseley's staff officers, Colonel J D Hamill-Stewart of the 11th Hussars who had done some service in the Sudan. They dug him out of his club and he agreed to go although he had no time to pack or get his uniform. Gordon and he then travelled to Calais and then by the Brindisi Mail down to South Italy.

"Arrived Brindisi - fatiguing journey", Gordon wrote on a postcard to General Sir Dighton Probyn, an old friend. "As

HMG will not guarantee future good government it seems evacuation is the only thing that could be done. - One chance is that Zubair's friends may take me for hostage for his return! but it does not discomfort me and I feel cheery as to the future of the whole affair".

Back in London Brocklehurst was doing his best to pick up the pieces. Gordon had wired King Leopold, but there was a letter to be sent to his Minister, Colonel Stranch saying that his services were required for a few months in the Sudan - "I trust His Majesty will not be inconvenienced for these few months.....Please present my respects to His Majesty and apologise on my part for being unable to see him, which I hope to do in a short time."

Brocklehurst also had a postcard from Brindisi thanking him for registering Gordon's baggage. "I asked my brother to repay you - you did it all". Gordon seemed to bear no grudge against Brocklehurst for reluctantly deciding not to go with him and instead reinforced the debt he felt he owed him. In a letter to Marianne Brocklehurst from aboard the *SS Tagore* at sea off the coast of Candia. Gordon wrote:

"I got your address from your nephew Capt. Brocklehurst, who has been exceedingly kind to me; he is the cause of my going out and of all this storm.

I am glad to go, for I expect things will be better for my visit, and I am glad that our Government will not suffer them reconquered, for such would be unjust, unless we at some time secured their future government which is too onerous a task to undertake."

There was an added postscript: "Your nephew is a most kind fellow to me; you have little idea the bother he has all for me."

In the meantime Brocklehurst, primed by Gordon, contributed the following leading article to *'The Times'* on

Monday 21st January 1884: It is such a succinct description of the situation in the Sudan that I have quoted it in full.

"It is impossible to exaggerate the feelings of relief and satisfaction universally inspired by the knowledge that General Gordon has undertaken the pacification of the Sudan.

"A great step in advance is felt to have been taken when the Cabinet asked for his assistance and his character is a guarantee not only that everything will be done in the best and most effective way, but also that nothing will induce him to swerve from the tenour of the policy which he has publicly declared to be, in his opinion, the right one. We are able to give some authentic particulars concerning plans every detail of which is of high public interest.

"General Gordon, with his accustomed directness of action, will go straight to Suakim via the Canal. At Suez he will meet Sir Evelyn Baring, with whom he will come to an understanding on the co-operation of the English authorities in Egypt, so far as that may be necessary. It is characteristic of him, and also significant as an indication of the drift of events, that he insists on being regarded as the representative of England, not of the Egyptian Government and will take pains to avoid interviews, however harmless in themselves which might by any chance give colour to a contrary view of his mission. On reaching Suakim he will at once bring into play his knowledge of local characters and his personal influence with local chiefs. The road from Suakim to Berber passes through the domains of the Hadendowa and Bisharin tribes, with both of whom he is on friendly terms. Moussa, the chief of the Hadendowa tribe, whose headquarters are at Filik, some 200 miles to the south of Suakim, is under a great personal obligation to General Gordon who, when formerly in the Sudan, saved two of Moussa's sons from the death to which they had been condemned by the Egyptian authorities for taking part in a raid upon another tribe. The Hadendowa chief will be summoned to Suakim and under his escort General Gordon expects to proceed at once to Khartoum. When there he will assemble the heads of the neighbouring tribes and announce to them that he has come on the part of the English Government to restore to them their liberty and to remove the swarms of unpaid soldiers and adventurers of various kinds who have been the curse of the country. He will have another communication to make, which they may find less agreeable, but which they will have been taught by experience to respect. He will inform them that the slave trade must positively cease, and that as soon as he has finished what he has to do in the Soudan he is going round to the Congo to deal with slavery at its headquarters.

General Gordon thus regards his engagement with the King of the Belgians as merely postponed, not by any means as abandoned. He does not anticipate being longer than four or five months in the Soudan and on his return will proceed at once to the Congo.

Meantime King Leopold is naturally very much disappointed at losing his tried agent when everything was on the point of complete settlement. He has asked the English Government, in a memorial presented by General Gordon himself, to send him a couple of English officers to act ad interim on the Congo. The King has strong claims upon English courtesy and gratitude and the enterprise itself is one which commands the warm sympathies of the English people. It may be hoped, therefore, that the Government will find means to comply with a request which conveys a national compliment. There is no nation in Europe which could not furnish volunteers for such work as this, and every facility should be given for English officers to associate themselves with the enterprise to which General Gordon is pledged. He perceives, and the rest of the world will in due course discover, that affairs on the Congo and on the Nile are inseparably connected, and that the mission of civilisation cannot be adequately carried out on one river if it is shirked on the other. This perception has undoubtedly had considerable influence in forcing his own views as to the proper policy of this country in the Soudan, which as is well known, do not include the abandonment of Khartoum.

Whatever the restrictions which the Government still sees fit to place upon its action and aims, it will probably find in the long run that Egypt cannot be arbitrarily limited to the delta. Ministers have been driven from one position after another by the force of events, and they have not yet by any means reached finality. At first they would have nothing to do with the Soudan, and apparently contemplated the abandonment even of Suakim. A pretty strong expression of public opinion has convinced them that this would not be tolerated and the Red Sea coast is now to be retained. When the matter comes to be more closely investigated it will be found that Khartoum can no more be thrown away than Suakim. It is not only the key of Lower Egypt and an indispensable post of observance on the Nile,but it is also the key of the Soudan, whether for the development of commerce or the suppression of slavery. General Gordon is commissioned to report upon the military situation, and his grip of facts is too thorough to leave very much doubt as to what his report will be. If Khartoum is not held by a just and wise government it must become a den of thieves and a centre for all the infamous transactions of slave driving. It is of far too much importance to be let alone, and it can hardly be supposed by the most fanatical believers in autonomy that the adjacent tribes can be formed into a stable and settled government even by the genius of General Gordon. Whatever Power holds Cairo and Suakim will be compelled by the necessity of things, to maintain order at Khartoum.

This does not in any way hinder General Gordon from providing for the evacuation of the Soudan, with the exception of the seaboard. Indeed, such an evacuation of the country to the south of Khartoum is a condition precedent of all healthy re-organisation. A mass of Egyptian soldiers and officials, variously estimated at from 25,000 to 40,000 men, has been let loose upon the country in the name of occupation. At one time they were paid out of the revenue of Lower Egypt, but when Ismail's extravagant administration had met its inevitable doom of bankruptcy it was held that the Soudan must be self-supporting. Under a strong and honest government even this might have been possible, but the Egyptian way of going to work was simply to cease paying the troops, leaving them under the control of corrupt officials to extract their own livelihood from the provinces they occupied. Evacuation of all that horde of lawless plunderers must undoubtedly be brought about before we can hope to see the Soudan settle down into any kind of tranquillity.

But if that were effected, there is every reason to believe that the Mahdi would at once cease to be formidable and that a thoroughly honest and capable administration at Khartoum would very speedily win the respect of the natives and exert over them all the influence that it is necessary for the rulers of Egypt to wield.

The difference between Khartoum and Wady Halfa as the boundary of Egypt is not merely one of degree. It is a difference in kind. Khartoum commands the fertile country beyond the desert, Wady Halfa does not. Khartoum brings our influence to bear upon the slave trade, while at Wady Halfa we are out of touch altogether. Khartoum is capable of being the centre of an active and healthy commerce, which Wady Halfa, or indeed any point we may choose between the delta and the junction of the White and Blue Niles, must remain commercially barren. In a word, Khartoum and Suakim constitute a frontier across which a state may hold relations with the African interior, while any more northerly point is, and must remain, a mere stopping-place in the desert.

We venture to anticipate that when General Gordon has got rid of the rapacious and disorderly elements which now provoke the resentment of the natives throughout the vast territory vaguely known as the Soudan, he will find that the peaceable occupation of Khartoum is a very simple affair, and its abandonment a very hazardous one.

Meantime, however, his appointment to investigate matters on the spot has relieved the apprehensions of immediate misery which were rapidly becoming acute. The public will now be able to await with greater equanimity the development of events, and the Cabinet itself will undoubtedly discuss its domestic policy this week with a freedom from anxiety to which it would otherwise have been a stranger."

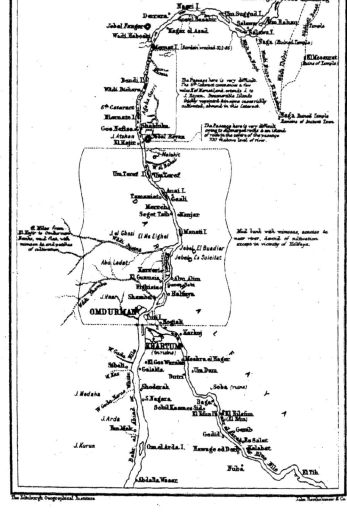

CHAPTER SEVEN

Knowing that Gordon had intended to sail down the Red Sea coast to Suakim, Brocklehurst was surprised to receive a letter from him at General Sir Evelyn Wood's house in Cairo. Gordon and Stewart had arrived at Port Said only to be met by Evelyn Wood with instructions from Baring for Gordon to change his plans and divert to Cairo for consultations and to pay his respects to the Khedive.

They were taken by steam launch to Ismalia and from there by fast train to the capital.

"I was taken to Baring same night and on next day saw Tewfik [the Khedive] and was 'abject' (i.e. apologised, Stewart gave this title)" Gordon wrote. The apology was for calling Tewfik 'a snake' in his interview with Stead, which had offended the Khedive when he read it in *The Times*.

"We have had two days long weary talks and tonight I go to Korosko and reach dv Khartoum in 19 days", he wrote to Brocklehurst .[dv - deo volente - God willing - was frequently used by Gordon, especially at this time.]

It had been decided by Baring that Gordon was not just going to act as an observer for the British Government, but was to be made Governor-General again while he carried out the evacuation and settled a new administration to govern the Sudan. 'A distinct departure from the terms on which he had left England'.

"Tewfik gave me the *firman* on the same sofa as Ismail gave me the same *firman* as Governor-General when I went up with you in 1877. Sharif Pasha being also present on both occasions. I was as civil as I could be to Tewfik."he told Brocklehurst.

In the meantime he had unexpectedly encountered Zubair, the infamous slave trader who had been kept in exile from the Sudan for nine years, following his insurrections in Bahr el Ghazal and Darfur. Gordon, who had once regarded him as a sworn enemy, suddenly had the premonition that Zubair would be the right man to rule the Sudan. 'He would be accepted on all sides and....end the Mahdi in a couple of months'. On the other hand he knew that Zubair was full of hatred towards him - holding him responsible for the death of his son Suleiman at the hands of Gessi and for the confiscation of his property. Gordon therefore proposed that they should meet in the presence of Baring and Nubar (the prime minister).

"Zubair and I were had up - before Baring and Nubar and we pleaded our causes. What the two, Baring and Nubar decided, I do not know. I am precious tired of long wearisome talks," he told Brocklehurst, "yet I have often thought of you, for you have been a kind friend to me"

At the time he claimed to be 'quite comfortable about my mission' but he was less so when he found that it had been decided that Zubair could not go to Khartoum until Gordon had come back safely - there was information that Zubair was liable to pursue his blood feud and have Gordon killed. To send them both to Khartoum seemed to Baring at the time to be as mad and dangerous as Gordon's idea of riding off into the desert to meet the Mahdi.

Gordon and Stewart then left Cairo on the night train for the rail head at Assiout, where a special steamer had been laid on by Thomas Cook to take them up the Nile to Korosko. Gordon took advantage of the eight-day journey to start sending a stream of telegrams to Baring setting out his plans.

Their use of the telegraph underlined the difference between him and Baring - Gordon used the telegraph as a form of conversation, setting down thoughts as they came into his head and often contradicting them in the next telegraph, whereas Baring, who was very precise and orderly, would not have considered even drafting a paper, let alone a telegraph, until it was clear in his mind. Gordon's telegrams, sometimes numbering 20 to 30 a day, soon began to exasperate him.

Gordon and his party reached Korosko on the 2nd February and set off on camels across the wild and desolate Nubian desert, and Brocklehurst finally caught up with his progress when he received a letter from him on the 8th February from Abu Hamid.

"I got here yesterday, through that terrible desert" Gordon wrote. "It was fearfully cold at night and ditto hot by day. From the number of applications I have received for higher pay, and for appts.[appointments] it would seem that the people here have no idea of panic, for if they did, they would never make such applications. I have ignored the existence of any rebellion, and I hope to meet many of the chiefs of the Mahdi's army at Khartoum, there is no chance of his leaving Kordofan. We are going to have a big conclave at Khartoum on 25 Feby. I hope that the country will be quiet in a month."

After more than four years Gordon found himself riding camels again. "I got on a fresh camel near here, a bull-necked brute, and off he went full speed with me." he wrote to

Brocklehurst."I was in a state of mind, not for my bones, but had I fallen, it would have been a very bad omen and done much harm with these superstitious people. I am glad to say I kept my seat and I shall indulge in no more of these displays.The people are very civil, and glad to see me, they are in no panic at all. I expect one will be obliged to drive the Egyptian Element out and that it is now question of how to get them down, it is a queer state of affairs."

After three days riding along the Nile he reached Berber which was the second city of the Sudan where they continued to be welcomed. A short note to Brocklehurst reported "a very good reception."

There were a packet of telegrams for them there waiting to be deciphered, including one from Baring expressly forbidding Gordon from attempting to visit the Mahdi. However, the most alarming news was that Valentine Baker Pasha, Sir Samuel Baker's brother had been defeated by the rebel Osman Digna at El Teb, near Suakim. If Suakim fell the road between Berber and the Red Sea, which was the shortest route for the evacuation of Khartoum, was effectively closed, and Suakim was also a vital stage on the British sea route to India.

Gordon decided to make public the fact that the Sudan was in future to be independent of Egypt, hoping to spur the local leaders to form a local government. At first it seemed as if giving the Sheikhs their independence was popular. "I think Berber Mudiarat are quite content with their future arrangements", he wrote to Brocklehurst "and are precious glad to be rid of the old lot whom they heartily despised and hated. It has been a true pleasure to have seen these people again".

In fact, as Gordon himself admitted later, this move was a mistake. The tribes were fearful of being exposed to the Mahdi when Egypt had departed and instead themselves began to gravitate towards the Mahdi.

Gordon continued up the Nile to Khartoum where he arrived on the 18th February to a rapturous welcome. "Five years absence had done nothing to efface the people's memory of his firmness, his liberality and the magnetism of his name." Arrangements were made at once to start the evacuation of Egyptian soldiers, as well as women and children, while Gordon attempted to rebuild the government and reorganise the army.

"I am, thank God, all right", he wrote to Brocklehurst on 3rd March "and though I have a good deal of bother, yet dv I hope to pull through. I want Zubair up here very much. He alone can form the future Government of these lands. We never could govern them now the people are far gone in the way of anarchy. He will like it for he is the master of intrigue".

Gordon was more than ever convinced that Zubair was necessary to secure the evacuation of Khartoum and create a stable government in the Sudan. As Churchill later surmised "the Pasha was vile but indispensable". For once Baring supported Gordon, but the government in London were divided and fearful of public opinion because of Zubair's reputation as the greatest slave hunter who had ever existed.

"Gordon hammered at Baring to send him Zubair" wrote Reginald Wingate, who was ADC to Evelyn Wood at the time, "and Baring hammered at London. The series of telegrams between Gordon, Baring and London is painful reading. For the British Cabinet not only categorically refused to permit the dispatch of Zubair, but refused, in spite of urgent and almost desperate explanations by Baring, to recognise that Gordon was in danger."

In his book *"The White Nile"* Alan Moorehead blames Gordon in part for the failure of the Zubair initiative. "The public might have come round", he said "but Gordon undid all Baring's tactful and persistent work. In a rage at the delay he sent for Frank Power - *The Times* correspondent and British Consul in Khartoum - and laid before him the whole story of the negotiations with Zubair". When this was published a storm of protest broke out in England with the Anti-Slavery Society at the fore and all the 'goody-goodies' behind them. Armed with this ammunition the Tory party opposed the government and on the 16th March the final "No" came through.

It seems ironic that the Anti-Slavery Society were in part responsible for Gordon's death for as Wingate wrote sometime after the events "If anyone knew what the slave trade was and was sincerely devoted to its suppression that one was Gordon".

Ten days before learning of the Zubair decision Gordon wrote reassuringly to Brocklehurst. "I am all right for the present and if it was not for the emissaries of Mahdi I should be all right for some time, but there is a painful uncertitude as to how the peasants will act, which disturbs one's quiet, for I am so weak that I cannot act agst. them, however small the rising may be. I hope in time, if allowed me, to convince the people the Mahdi is not in a position to help them, for from all accounts he is distrustful of his own people and fearful of the tribes around him, and that there is not the least fear of his issuing out of his city [El Obeid], where he has established not even the pretence of a government."

Brocklehurst was apparently still taking care of some of Gordon's affairs as he added to the letter "I am glad you saw HRH the Prince and the Duke and told them about King

Leopold. I will dv be back in Sept. and <u>will go to Congo</u>, for I cannot desert HM after all his kindness."

In the meantime Gordon found any plans he attempted to make for the evacuation of Khartoum up the Nile were refused. Brocklehurst reported to his Aunt Emma that Stead had printed a letter from Gordon in the *Pall Mall Gazette*, saying he had demanded orders if he was to cut and run, which he proposed doing by going up the Nile with the whole garrison to the Equatorial Provinces and home via the Congo. "He is a gallant old boy isn't he?" Brocklehurst wrote, "but he'll stay now and hold the place I expect."

In support of his friend Brocklehurst added a copy of Gordon's letter to him about Zubair in a letter to *The Times* where it was "put in a prominent place and I am glad of it as I hope it will draw attention to the way Sir E Baring is <u>assisting</u> Gordon".

Meanwhile the net was beginning to draw tighter round Khartoum. The tribes to the north of the city, which Zubair could have controlled, now declared for the Mahdi and blocked the Egyptian traffic on the Nile. The telegraph line was cut and Berber fell the next month. From March 1884 to January 1885 Khartoum was cut off from the world.

Determined to keep in touch with Gordon somehow Brocklehurst lost no time in collecting a group of his friends together and worked out an ingenious plan to smuggle letters and English newspapers and reports to him through the Mahdi's lines. Using funds mainly supplied by Baroness Burdett-Coutts, a close friend of Gordon's, an English merchant from Morocco called Curtis was paid £700 for the dangerous mission. Disguised as an Arab with the name of Abd-al-Qadir he went first to Cairo where he had the papers shrunk photographically to the size of a postage stamp so that they could be hidden about his person- on the point of his spear, in his turban, even up his bottom. This was highly dangerous work. The Mahdi had spies everywhere - and the ring of steel around Khartoum was almost impossible to penetrate. But Curtis got through - time and again. Seven times he made the perilous journey through the rebel lines to Khartoum with his precious mail until he began to be recognised and came under suspicion, so that his last two mail runs ended up in the Mahdi's camp.

We know that at least some of the messages and letters got through to Gordon because he later enclosed one in his final letter to Brocklehurst with the last dispatch. There is an apocryphal story that Gordon could not read the minute writing on the shrunken papers as he had no magnifying glass - but discovered that by placing a water-filled carafe in the sun over the messages he could decipher most of them.

Two messages which only reached as far as the Mahdi's camp were a letter to Gordon from Macmillans the publishers saying that the sales of his book "Reflections in Palestine" amounted to about 5,500 copies and it had been well received by the press, and a telegram from the Private Secretary to the King of the Belgians - 'the King sends expressions of deepest interest and of best wishes'.

One of Brocklehurst's own letters to Gordon, which we will later discover did reach him in Khartoum said: "My dear Friend, I sincerely hope you will get this and the accompanying papers, which will tell you all the news. My wife sends very kind regards. Hoping all will come right and we shall meet again soon, Yours always John F Brocklehurst."

Baroness Burdett-Coutts sent Gordon a copy of her letter

published in *The Times* in which she said she had been entreated to organise, by public subscription, a volunteer movement to attempt the relief of General Gordon. Poor men had offered their support 'a French workman offers you his 20 francs worth with an English lady who would send £5,000'. "General Gordon looks to the equator as his only point of refuge" she wrote, noting with some "bitterness of heart" that it was not to England that he turned for hope in his abandonment.

In spite of many such public and private appeals the Government remained obdurate. Gladstone was not prepared to admit that Gordon was cut off or in any kind of danger - he was just "hemmed in" for the time being.

In fact, few men could have been conducting the siege conditions in Khartoum better than Gordon. In his biography '*Gordon, The Man Behind the Legend*' John Pollock reports that "Gordon was in his element, his skills and experience as commander, engineer and administrator at full stretch......As the siege pressed more heavily Gordon leased the empty Austrian church and mission, the strong stone building next to the Palace, and made it the arsenal. When the Nile waters sank with the coming of summer he extended the fortified ditch to the White Nile and placed a chain across the Blue Nile linked to mined barges and garrisoned the uncovered sandbanks. He had already fortified his little 'penny' steamers into gunboats and sent them up and down the river to bombard rebel positions."

When the treasury ran out of funds he printed his own paper money - signing some 50,000 bank notes personally before the printers found a way to reproduce his signature. He ensured that the town's food supplies were being fairly distributed and, as one way to keep up morale, had metal stars made to reward good service.

"But all this time the dervishes were getting more and more troublesome" - in May Berber had fallen to the Mahdi and when news of this reached London over a month later the clamour for Gordon's rescue intensified. Lord Hartington threatened to resign unless a relief expedition was sent to Khartoum. His resignation would have been enough to bring the government down and Gladstone was forced to give way at last.

On the 8th August it was announced that a military expedition would be sent to the Sudan and Parliament voted £300,000 for expenses. Gordon's old friend Lord Wolseley was selected to command the expedition.

CHAPTER EIGHT

Dear Brocklehurst. I have asked that you may be sent to Egypt on special services" read a letter from Wolseley dated the 27th August 1884. "Is this agreeable to you and when would you be able to start?"

Wolseley was hand-picking the officers who he wanted to serve with him on the Gordon Relief Expedition and knowing how close Brocklehurst was to Gordon felt he would want to be included in the force. There was no shortage of volunteers, including the Prince of Wales, who had pleaded vainly for permission to join the expedition and serve under Wolseley. In fact so many of the top names in the Army had been chosen that some of the Radicals in the government denounced the whole expedition as a 'social stunt'.

A letter from Lord Wolseley to the Prince of Wales reads "I have asked for Captn Brocklehurst of the Blues, He is a great friend of General Gordon's and has been in the Soudan with him. He is a first rate man to work and I am glad to have some men from Your Rl Highness's Household Cavalry."

Louie was distraught at Wolseley's request. Having successfully persuaded Brocklehurst not to go to Khartoum with Gordon the last thing she wanted was for him to go to Egypt again.

"It is all settled and my poor old man has to be ready to start next Tuesday tho' they don't think he will go till the Tuesday after" she wrote to his Aunt Emma. "Lord Wolseley made a point of his going and I suppose it is no use rebelling, but it is hard all the same to let him go again. Oh if he would but leave that horrid army. I know you will be sorry for us. You see it is not as if he was keen for military glory - he really doesn't care a bit about it and I'm sure I don't. I am afraid I am a very unheroic person." she confessed.

There was also some confusion about what exactly Brocklehurst's position was going to be.

"The orders came yesterday and they say he goes on 'special service with status of deputy assistant adjutant quartermaster general' but what that implies I do not know or anyone else" Louie told Aunt Emma, who wrote in her diary, "We hear Johnny is invited to join the Egyptian expedition as 'Deputy assistant adjutant Quarter Master General'. We have cause I think to be proud of him. General Lowe, one of our finest cavalry officers said to Philip [Emma's brother] a short time ago: 'Your nephew is as good a soldier as ever wore the Queen's uniform, and as good a fellow as he is a soldier'."

William [her eldest brother] writes: "The news was officially announced in *The Times* of yesterday but the post he is to occupy is not set forth. It is however one of good position, and it seems to me that there is a certain amount of Diplomatic employment attached to it which speaks well for the opinion in which he is held by those who are sending him. I do honestly think he will do his duty well in whatever capacity he may be called upon to act.

About six weeks ago I spent a Sunday morning with him at his house at Albert Gate. I was much struck with the steadied thoughtful style he has got into, and I found he had been working hard to prepare himself for some such sort of employment. He was studying French and German and had become pretty proficient. I have no doubt he has his foot on the first stair of the ladder and that he will make a mark for our family name whenever opportunity offers itself."

In fact the exact nature of the job was to prove far more mundane. While this and his final departure were being worked out in England the situation in Khartoum was becoming critical.

Desperate for news, and concerned that unless some outside help arrived within the next month or two Khartoum would fall, Gordon decided to send Stewart down the Nile on the steamer *Abbas* with dispatches urgently appealing for immediate help. Frank Power, *The Times* correspondent, was to go with him so that he could once again contact the newspaper, and the French consul and one or two Egyptian officials made up the party. A box of swords for Brocklehurst was included in the baggage, with the mail, and the cipher books, to allow Stewart to telegraph freely and also prevent them falling into the Mahdi's hands.

They steamed away safely on the 12th September. The Nile was now high and they were escorted by two armed steamers as they journeyed through the hostile tribes to more friendly territory.

At the time, Gordon did not know that the relief expedition had arrived in Cairo on the 9th September, and that while Wolseley set about moving his 7,000 men and their equipment across the desert Kitchener had gone ahead of the column and had established an intelligence post at Debba from where he was able to send runners in and out of Khartoum. In this way by the last week in September the news finally reached Gordon that relief was on its way.

The same week Brocklehurst left for the Sudan and in a letter to his Aunt Emma from Calais said: "I am off at last, Louie and I having left London this morning and we are breaking the journey here as it was too awkward to do so at Brussels. (Louie had earlier been promised that she would be allowed to go with him as far as Brussels). I go on by the mail tonight straight through to Trieste to meet the boat which I hear is so full that I shall be fortunate if I get standing room."

Later a letter followed from Louie on her return, saying that she had heard from Johnny at Corfu on his way to Alexandria. "The boat crowded with people of all nationalities. I know nothing of his movements yet as I only got a telegram when he arrived at Alexandria. This quarantine is so provoking, letters and everything having to go via Trieste makes the post two days longer. General Gordon seems to have achieved so much of his own prowess I can't help hoping the whole thing will be over much sooner than was anticipated. Is he not a splendid fellow?.......I do hope the rumour published today that Col. Stewart was killed at Berber is not true, it would be very sad after he has gone through the danger and discomfort of the siege to lose his life just as things are getting brighter."

In fact we know the rumour was only too true. Gordon himself first learnt of it in a letter from the Mahdi informing him that the steamer *Abbas* had been captured and Stewart killed. He did not want to believe it, but a message smuggled through from Kitchener confirmed the story.

We now know that shortly before reaching the village of Abu Hamed the *Abbas* had struck a rock in the Nile and been disabled. Stewart went ashore for help and met what he thought was a friendly sheikh who promised to take the party by camel overland. The sheikh invited them to a meal that night to which they went unarmed, relying on the rules of Arab hospitality. At a given signal they were set upon and murdered, both Stewart and Power putting up a fight, before the Arabs went aboard the *Abbas*, seizing the dispatches and cipher and killing all but 14 of the remaining passengers and crew. There were also a number of Greeks with Stewart, some of whom may have escaped.

By October Brocklehurst had arrived to join the Relief Expedition at Wady Halfa. "I am given a billet under Sir E Wood and am head of the Camel Depot which is in the desert away from the Camp. I have two English sergeants, a lot of Egyptians and a certain number of niggers to run the job. All camels are handed to me and I have to brand, sort and nurse them, so my time will be full I guess. I have got a tent and live by myself which I like best. Crowe is butler and housemaid and Abou Said, cook. Several messes have kindly offered to take me in. I have dined and had sundry meals with Ld. Wolseley, who is very kind and has told me to go to his boat whenever I like and I have only to turn up if I want a feed. General Earle and Col. Duncan have also been very kind and I like Sir E Wood very much.

I have got 3 sheep (the only ones in camp) 6 pigeons, 2 chickens and 1 pony (such a nice little beast) by way of a farm. I get up at about 4.30 am and go to bed at 8, except when I am dining out.

This is a dreary looking place - all sand with the exception of a strip close to the river where palm trees grow. It is all dust and glare everywhere else and everyone's eyes look so sore. There doesn't seem much game about but I caught a lovely scorpion under my bed yesterday. Everyone thinks it will be quite easy to get to Khartoum by boat or camel."

Meanwhile alone and waiting in Khartoum Gordon found comfort in the local wild life - a small female mouse took Stewart's place at table - "she comes and eats out of my plate without fear. Then there is the turkey-cock that has become so disagreeable that I had to put his head under his wing and swing him to and fro till he slept", he recorded in the journal which had become his safety valve and amusement - 'wild jottings, sometimes on telegraph forms and flimsy scraps of paper - sometimes heavily underlined or crossed out - sometimes decorated with oddly exact little maps and ribald caricatures - sometimes pathetic, ironical or recklessly unfair, but always absolutely honest.'

Telegrams were beginning to come through to him via Kitchener but of course they were in cipher and without the cipher which had gone with Stewart he could not read them.

A letter from the Mahdi claiming Stewart's capture and death enclosed a long list of all the papers which had been taken from the dead men, including details of the amount of food and ammunition remaining in Khartoum and a census of the number of soldiers in the garrison. Armed with this information the Mahdi had moved the bulk of his forces close to Omdurman on the western bank of the Nile and announced his intention to attack Khartoum. The final stage of the siege had begun.

Gordon still had plenty of ammunition but the food situation was critical. "If they (the British troops) don't come before 30 November the game is up and Rule Britannia", he wrote.

Back at Wady Halfa Brocklehurst was hard at work getting his 'location' shipshape. "I have today 145 camels. 94 of which are sick, 16 donkeys, 1 mule and six ponies" he told Louie by letter. "The camels are again divided into those for riding, those for carrying loads (titbits for self and friends) and isolated cases sick with mange, smallpox etc. I have 2 Europeans, 1 Sheikh and 13 blacks and 2 sheiks and 23 Berbury men. The camels are watered every two days and fed and exercised every day when, of course, the niggers mix everything up, riders, baggagers, sick beasts etc. Another thing I have to struggle with is to prevent the niggers feeding and watering the ponies as they do the camels. It is a maddening outfit but just suits me and I like it very much. I have at last got the camp pitched properly and make them keep it tidy which they think is a very funny fad of mine.

Five stray camels in my lines today, goodness knows where they have come from. I am expecting 300 or 400 more to sort today, also some 50 odd mules. I am getting very fond of my sheep, especially one black one, such a funny old party with lop ears and a sly look. He peeps at me round the corner of my tent when I am eating and takes great interest in me. I can never find heart to kill him.

I bought some camels from Beresford this morning and am negotiating for two horses with an Arab officer, they will be useful to someone later on and I believe I shall have to mount the heavy cavalry. I will telegraph if I can make any plans for you" he assured Louie.

By the end of October his depot was "quite smart and tidy" - except on odd days when everything went wrong with the niggers. "A lot of work is done. Backs dressed, all animals exercised, horses groomed, camels well scratched with curry combs (hideous is the row they make during the process), lines cleaned, feeding, watering, men paid and so on.

Keeping accounts, which are endless is the worst - This morning I gave over 45 mules, 13 donkeys, 6 camels and kit for same to different officers for private use. Then I have to take over 85 camels and lend some odd ones to different people who had orders for a mount. You don't know what a business it is, as I am responsible for every animal and every strap of the tackle belonging to them and I have to get an order and a receipt and a delivery voucher for everything, even a lent camel. There are still 104 sick camels in the camp to be nursed - there is the office to attend to, questions to answer at a moment's notice as to when some beast or article of kit came, went, was lent, or died, to say nothing of paying the men who were mostly hired before I came by different people on different wages and different rations. However, I delight in the job and am entirely my own master.

I cannot tell you any army news, you know more than I do, but I expect to go on shortly, as soon as I have cured and handed over my beasts to the Camel Corps etc."

Louie had been to stay with Aunt Emma at Sudeley Castle and Brocklehurst wrote to his aunt, expressing his thanks for her kindness to his wife- "Poor little person, I daresay it sounds conceited but I know she is very much lost without me, and I am very glad it is so". Louie plagued with terrible headaches, which may have been migraine, had cut off all her hair and in consequence said she looked 'no end of a guy'.

"I expect now to be permanently attached to the camels," he told Aunt Emma. So much for the belief that this was to have been a 'diplomatic' posting. "The beautiful boat Louisa, which I bought with your £100 will be used by someone else. When I bought her I had no idea anything but boats were going to be used, or I should not have done so. She is quite a character on the river, everyone doing their best to get on her (though there are strict orders against private boats) and now she floats cockily at Gezera having made nothing of the Bab el Kabeer, the worst cataract on the Nile, and well known I expect to the MBs.

Of course we do not know half as much here as you do in England of what is going on, but I expect to leave in about a fortnight, perhaps as sicknurse to camels, but I cannot say .....the outdoor work is very nice, but its them accounts".

He wrote of his impatience at the delays to Louie - "Oh dear, nearly 10 weeks since he went and nothing done - things seem to hang on so", she said.

By the 13th December Gordon estimated that he could hold out in Khartoum for another 10 days. He spent more and more of his time on the Palace roof where with his telescope he could scan the horizons and see as far as the Northen Fort at Omdurman, now cut off from Khartoum by the Mahdi's forces who had their guns in position round the town, and every day the shelling and rifle fire grew heavier.

On that day Gordon wrote in his diary: " NOW MARK THIS if the Expeditionary Force and I ask for no more than 200 men does not come in 10 days the town may fall and I have done the best for the honour of my country. Good-bye C.G.Gordon.

You send me no information, although you have lots of money C.G.G."

He then bundled up the papers of his journal - the telegraph forms, the pieces of tissue paper, the little maps he had made and the pen-and-ink sketches - secured them up in a cloth and wrote on the wrapper. 'Events at Khartoum. Gen Gordon's Journal. No secrets as far as I am concerned. To be pared down if published' C.G.Gordon'.

The package was handed to the captain of the *Bordein* together with letters to his sister Augusta and his closest friends. They included one to Brocklehurst, thanking him for the messages he had succeeded in getting smuggled through to Khartoum by Curtis, and including a sample one to show that the messages had got through.

My dear Brocklehurst Thanks, many to you, Mrs Brocklehurst, the "Foreign Office" (Miss Marianne Brocklehurst and Miss Booth), Brett and Hobart for the kind efforts you have made for me and the people up here. I sent you a box of swords etc. by Stewart, who, though we have no positive news I fear is lost, and with him the box.

I am not coming to England again (if I ever get out which is not very sure) but shall go to Brussels and so on to Congo, glad to get quiet there. You must come to Brussels for 2 days and we will go to Waterloo. What a business it has been, poor Gladstone's Govt, they must love me. I will have nothing to do with them and will not let them pay my expenses up here, but will get King of B to pay them.

Excuse a hurried scrawl. I will telegraph you when I get out of this. Believe me with kindest regards and thanks to you, Mrs Brocklehurst, the "F.O." and Brett and Hobart.

Yours sincerely

C.G. Gordon.

On the 15th December the *Bourdein* steamed off carrying this final dispatch from Gordon and left, under heavy fire, for Metemmeh..

CHAPTER NINE

It was the end of December 1884 before the advance guard of the expedition reached the Nile at Korti and was ready to start the final advance to Khartoum. Wolseley was following a plan proposed by Gordon for one column to follow the Nile on an eastward loop past Abdu Hamel and Berber, while the other column under Sir Herbert Stewart would march across the desert to Metemmeh to meet up with the steamers.

Brocklehurst, well in the vanguard, spent December setting up and moving his remount depot, which was to follow the Camel Corps, with five per cent of spare beasts and a supply of artificers, material to mend broken saddles and physic for sick camels. "In fact a sort of moving saddler's shop and livery stable combined" he told Louie. "Five per cent of spare camels for the Corps alone means something like 300 camels, so it will be a biggish job and a Capt.Hempshill has been attached to me as junior for which I am glad.

"I am going to have a sale of sorebacked camels in the village and I shall play auctioneer myself - so you see I'm having a bit of fun. I hope to have a day or two quiet to get ready for my march - I have been fitting out as well as I can as I shall be unattached and have to look out for myself. I am going out now to take my treasures to a field of green dhurra for a little salad for the good of their health, it is about 2 miles off."

Later he reported that 29 camels had sold well at the auction. "It was much harder work than I expected, but the natives were very funny and paid me in every sort of coin."

He was already the subject of a commendatory letter from Lord Wolseley to the Prince of Wales "the essence of a good officer is to do well whatever he is given to do, and I have always found that none enter more cordially into this view of matters than the officers under Your Royal Highness's Command in the Household Cavalry. Captain Brocklehurst of the Blues is now in charge of a camel remount Depot and two others in the Brigade are doing excellent work with the boats".

"The Times" special correspondent in Wady Halfa in an article on 'The Tactics of the Camel Corps' was equally fulsome; 'there can be no doubt that an immense amount of the success of the Expedition will be due to the zeal, pains and patience bestowed on the remount depot here by Captain Brocklehurst.... I have seen enough of the working to give the assurance that if untiring energy and the determination to do thoroughly with his might what has been committed into his hands are of any use in the struggle it will be performed to the entire satisfaction of everyone, from the General downwards. It is a highly responsible position - no sinecure - for one man and the task is not an easy one'.

By the time this appeared in the newspaper Brocklehurst had begun his journey to the front with a two mile long string of camels and mules. His letters to Louie, in their envelopes postmarked 'Nile Expedition - no stamps available', were copied and circulated around the Brocklehurst family and give a graphic account of his situation.

"December 6th - Bivouacked in the desert, no tents, clump of palm trees, a few huts. My vet, sub-sergeant, 66 niggers, 200 camels and 2 horses - a veritable Bedouin do I feel. We have been five days getting here - marching from daylight until about 4 pm over the most cruel desert - black rocks, deep red sand, small hills shaped like pyramids every now and then, but so dreary and tomblike.

The camels in a long string, heavily laden, though they are sick, as I have to carry food for man and beast for 14 days - and water too sometimes, in kegs, when we cannot get back to the Nile in one day's march. We slide along slowly and silently about one mile an hour - then one comes to the Nile and it looks like Paradise with its bit of green, but it does not follow that one can water the camels as the banks are so bad.

This desert journeying is no joke and is ticklish work unless your water supply is very carefully seen to and guarded. We have just had two days march without water. Last night the kegs were all put close to my bed to prevent the natives stealing it - I served it out to them on halting and it was a treat to see the poor beggars drink, muddy and hot as it was.

We had an awful long hot grind to get back to the river tonight and one camel died, poor beast, but I don't think it was from exhaustion. I have to be very careful about the camels' saddles keeping in their places as nearly all of them have sore backs and I don't want them to get any worse. Natives, of course, never look to anything and I find camel after camel with his saddle anywhere but where it ought to be. However, I have made such free use of my whip (which is strictly against orders) that I think they are getting a bit more careful.

December 7th - Have been hard at work all morning sorting out the worst backs and selecting others less bad, also inventing a saddle that is not going to gall. 7pm (about - all watches have gone pop) did a nice little march along the Nile and we are now bivouacked on its bank, such a pretty spot, the deep blue of the river and its fringe of green set off by the weird looking desert of rocks and sand on each side. My saddles worked very well, but my poor sick charges are tired and I don't know how they will stand the long journey tomorrow, but I shall give them a whole holiday at Saket el Abd where there is camel grass growing - I have had nothing to eat for nearly 12 hours (though plenty of tea and tobacco) and our frizzle is ready, so goodnight.

December 8th - Saket el Abd - and of course no grass, so I shall grind on again tomorrow. We started this morning about 2 hours before daybreak but I fitted the saddles first (130 of them) by the light of the moon and hard work it was as the bad smells from their sores were simply appalling. I use corn sacks folded Yankee fashion under the saddles and their backs are certainly better.

I had a grand shave when I got in and my hair cut and tonight I am going to sleep under a palm tree - a very little one, but a tree is a tree out here, I can tell you. There is a sort of coarse grass growing here and there and all the camels are out grazing with me sitting on a mound to see they don't go far - my sergeant does likewise on another mound."

While Brocklehurst's camel convoy wound its way slowly across the desert Gordon was attempting to rally the people in Khartoum. The Palace itself was now under fire. Gordon had no definite news of the relief and could not understand why a small number of troops could not be sent up to Halfaya "and thus let their presence be felt". He himself remained indomitable. "Go tell all the people in Khartoum that Gordon fears nothing, for God has created him without fear."

Just as Gordon was without definite news of the relief expedition Wolseley was equally ignorant of the true state of affairs in Khartoum. On December 30th one of Gordon's runners came into Wolseley's camp at Korti with a message written on a piece of paper the size of a postage stamp which read "Khartoum all right 12.12.84 C.G.Gordon." This message may have been intended as a gesture of confidence to deceive the Arabs, as the runner also reported verbally that food supplies in Khartoum were running very low and the expedition should come as quickly as possible. But far from urging the swift arrival of a small force he also asked for plenty of troops and warned that Berber should be overtaken. Wolseley believed that both messages were genuine and continued to prepare for the advance with caution rather than speed.

Back in the desert Brocklehurst said he had had no communication with the outside world for 14 days and had just arrived at Fakh el bent after about 14 hours of desert marching. "I was determined to try and get across from Kobak (though I carried water in case of accidents). I started about 3 hours before first light and just did it."

He had had "a bad day" he wrote to Louie. "Every saddle and every nigger seemed bent on teasing me and my temper was atrocious - It was awfully cold when we started and you know what cold niggers are worth poor things, but it is dark now and everything is more or less hitched up so my temper is beginning to cool a little and I've been trying not to let the sun go down on my wrath by making friends again with the darkies." On the bright side he had shot a sand grouse from the top of his camel with his revolver - "a beastly fluke".

"I hope to get into Dongola now in 3 or 4 days - no more night marching as the moon is down. This morning we got off again as soon after daylight as possible and are now working our slow way southwards, hoping to arrive at Hafir tonight (I am writing on my camel!). We are cutting off a bend of the river so are again in the desert, but all morning we were on the Nile bank and very pretty it was at the Cataract of Hanneck with its old ruined Turkish Castle.

I hope to find letters at Dongola as the post travels on the other bank at a trot - the reason we have had such a lonesome march is because the troops don't come this side of the river as no forage depots have been formed this side. As it is the most level road I thought better to come by it as we had to carry all our own forage for the journey - that in the depots being all wanted for the mounted corps and convoys.

I wish you could drop down here to see us all wiggle waggling along - it would make you laugh. A large man has just passed me sitting on a very small jackass which also carried two large sacks on which sat his little wife (about your size) sitting behind him and clinging round his waist with all her might. Yesterday a nice brown young woman came walking by my camel, trying to sell me some milk. Her clothes were scanty but her figure was not, she was well developed <u>very.</u>

I haven't had my clothes off for 3 days and really must have a tub tonight, tho' how to make time I don't know - that is time before the sun goes down. It gets so cold after dark that I'm afraid of chills, no I'll be dirty first (nice sentiment but true)."

By December 15th he had arrived at Dongola "having had a great morning amongst the camels, clearing up, sorting etc. - overhauled the natives little bundles and found a good deal of Her Majesty's property which rather annoyed them. It was a large village we stopped at last night and some natives came to be doctored, mostly for eyes, so I made some galarde lotion for them in a gourd and operated on a little boy, using a feather, to show them how to do it. His father held him but he managed to give me some vigorous kicks with his little bare feet."

By the time he arrived at Dongola Brocklehurst found that everyone else had cleared out to a place 40 miles away - Handak - and he had orders to move on there too. In the meantime he was glad to find a letter from Louie and one from his brother-in-law, Tom Fitzwilliam. "I think myself this will be a longish job and it's no use you doing anything about coming out until you hear from me", he warned Louie.

In the meantime he was stuck at Dongola with no drivers for his camel train and was ordered to go on to Handak alone. His former drivers were Dongolese men who having reached their home were in no mood to march off again. Persuasion from Brocklehurst, with some forward pay to conclude the bargain, had helped to change their minds until one of their Sheikhs went and complained to the Mudir (the great Mudir) that they were being forced to leave home again.

"So down comes a great swell on a white mule with all my men and their Sheikh to enquire into the matter", he wrote to Louie. "This ended in the Sheikh being corbashed in front of my tent while I and the Mudir drank coffee and smoked. The Sheikh was then let go and ordered to take his men with me to Handak. But he began intriguing again, so I had him put in prison and a fresh Sheikh appointed, and I expect now he rather wishes he hadn't. Am writing this on camel back so please excuse faults", he added.

At Dongola he had been joined by Conductor Sheppard with 30 camels and artificers, and the forge and kit for repairing saddlery which was to form part of his establishment - the Moveable Remount Depot. "A conductor though not an officer is nearly so and I have made him a member of the mess and I am going to make him manage it - he seems a very nice fellow".

The Kababish here are very good looking big fellows with fine perfectly straight noses - their hair taken back from their forehead and plaited in little tails quite high up to the head. They are a very powerful tribe, numbering some four milllion. We passed the place yesterday where the Mahdi was born (2 huts and a palm tree) and his people now live there. It didn't look like a place to produce all this bother".

Handak was the crossing point for all the troops from the other side of the river who had to be refitted with camels, so he was busier than ever "I am not going on just at present but am to stay here and buy as many camels as I can - up to 200. I was Commanding Officer here until today but thank goodness Major Sandworth has arrived to do that part of it. Camel buying is a very poor amusement and takes a lot of time.

Xmas the day after tomorrow and we are straining every nerve to have a plum pudding which will probably make us all very ill. This place is in a deep belt of palm trees and is the first bit of shade I have had since I came into the country - there is lots of good food here, native bread, eggs, mutton, vegetables, milk, butter etc. and we do very well.

These infernal niggers will keep bringing me camels to buy that I have rejected the day before and I have to be very careful not to be taken in as then my character as a wise man would be gone."

The camels were soon needed. At the beginning of January Sir Herbert Stewart had begun his advance to Khartoum with 100 British troops and on the 2nd January he set up an outpost at Jakdul Wells before returning to Korti for a further 1600 men and 2,400 camels. Brocklehurst was sent for in a hurry to march to Korti with 480 camels.

When he next wrote to Louie he had been at Korti for a week with a shifting number of camels in the depot of from 700 to 800. " There are never many fewer as the Corps take my good ones and give me those that are worn out - grain is short and labour more so, so I have to take them to a field about 2 miles off where they eat standing crops. It is a difficult game keeping the animals together and getting them home again as they are all loose. Yesterday I seized the head man of the district and kept him prisoner until he got me more men, he got very frightened and made great promises of more men for today - so I let him go and hope he will keep them.
So sorry to send such a scrap but you don't want to know all the bother and work here, only that I am well and at present have not made an irretrievable mess of anything!"

Louie, who was staying with her friend Blanche Waterford told Aunt Emma that both Blanche's brother and her brother-in-law were with Stewart's force. "I don't know whether Johnny is or not. We think they must have avoided Metemmeh and be marching straight for Khartoum, and, of course, with such small numbers they could not spare men and camels to escort messengers back, while if any disaster had happened it would certainly be known at once, as news, if there is any, flies like wildfire over the desert amongst the Arabs. So we have made up our minds not to expect to hear of them for some time, but it is trying work all the same and I do trust my old sweet is safe (for the present) at Korti, though no doubt he would prefer being in front."

Even as she wrote an Official Dispatch arrived at the War Office from General Lord Wolseley to the Secretary of State for War reporting that General Stewart had had a most successful encounter with about 10,000 of the Mahdi's forces near the Abu Klea Wells, some 22 miles on this side of Metemmeh. The enemy's force was collected from Berber, Metemmeh and Omdurman, "which place I regret to say prisoners' report was recently captured by the Mahdi; thus releasing men from there to fight Stewart."

"Stewart endeavoured to draw the enemy on to attack, but hesitated; so leaving all his impedimenta and camels under a guard of the Sussex Regiment - some mounted infantry - he moved forward in square, all men on foot, and passed around the left flank of enemy's position, forcing him to attack or be enfiladed.

Enemy wheeled to the left and delivered a well organised charge under a withering fire from our men. Square was unfortunately penetrated about its left rear, where Heavy Cavalry Camel Regiment stood, by sheer weight of numbers. The admirable steadiness of our men enabled a hand-to-hand combat to be maintained; while severe punishment was being inflicted on the enemy by all other parts of the square and the enemy was at last driven back under heavy fire from all sides.

The 19th Hussars then pushed forward to the Wells which were in our possession at 5 pm. The Arabs left no less than 800 dead round the square and prisoners report the number of wounded to be quite exceptional."

Among the British officers killed at Abu Klea was Colonel Fred Burnaby, 'a giant of a man', who had been a friend of Gordon's since first meeting him in Equatoria in 1875. It was Burnaby, who before the Relief Expedition had been organised, had attempted to raise a camel corps at his own expense to rescue Gordon from Khartoum, only to be turned down at the time by the assistant adjutant-general Sir Redvers Buller with the comment that "The man is not worth the camels".How ironic that Buller, now Chief of Staff on the Gordon Relief Expedition, was reputed to require 40 camels to carry his baggage which, included a good supply of 'fizz' (champagne), apparently a necessary prerequisite for his campaign life.

Having taken possession of Abu Klea Wells, Stewart's column resumed its march to Metemmeh to rendez-vous with the steamers, but at dawn on the 19th January, as they were in sight of the Nile, they came under further attack from the Arabs. In the fierce fighting which followed Sir Herbert Stewart was fatally wounded. With Burnaby among the earlier fatalities the command of the column now fell on Sir Charles Wilson, a Royal Engineers officer who was chief of the Intelligence Department and had never led troops in battle before.

Louie wrote to Aunt Emma to calm her forboding that Brocklehurst had been with Stewart's column. "Thank Heaven I don't think he can be with General Stewart as he telegraphed to me from Korti on Tuesday the 13th and as this battle was quite 6 days march beyond Korti he could not have got there by the 17th. It is very anxious work waiting for news now. I cannot think such small numbers as the army has been split up into can be very safe amongst such numbers of those savages who certainly mean fighting. I hope Ld Wolseley will recall Earle's colum, and let it combine with Sir H Stewart - and if only the Govt would order some Indian troops to Suakim to make a diversion that side."

Meanwhile back at Khartoum the Mahdi's soldiers fired a salute of 101 guns to signal a victory at Abu Klea, but from his rooftop terrace Gordon could see through his telescope that many of the women were weeping and guessed that the relief column had defeated the Arabs. By now he reckoned that they should have reached the steamers he had sent down the Nile. He rallied his troops, promising that the relief expedition would arrive the following day, or the one after and that they would have a year's pay for every day they hung on. The supply of maize in the town had long since been exhausted and every living animal - even the rats - had been killed and eaten. People were lying dead in the streets from starvation and the only food remaining was palm tree fibre and a species of gum.

From the roof of the Palace Gordon looked in vain for the puffs of smoke which would herald the arrival of his steamers bringing the relief force.

He would not have anticipated the two fatal days of delay, as Sir Charles Wilson ordered the steamers' engines to be overhauled and reconnaissance made along the Nile before setting out for Khartoum. When they did finally proceed on the 24th January the river had already fallen very low and the convoy was soon in difficulties in the Sixth Cataract.

The same fall in the level of the Nile was to provide the opportunity to end the 319 day siege of Khartoum. The Mahdi, who was afraid of the British soldiers now approaching up the river, was hesitating about whether to withdraw when he learned that the mud of the falling Nile had filled in part of the ditch on the south side of the town. Gordon had ordered it to be repaired, but his troops were too weak to carry out the work.

On the 25th January the Mahdi gave orders for the assault to be made on Khartoum the following morning. The moon set early and a great horde of some 40,000 Arabs crept up to the defences and invaded the city before daybreak, killing all in their path, men, women and children in six hours of brutal savagery.

The slaughter and pillaging was still going on when Sir Charles Wilson and his steamer born force appeared on the river on Gordon's birthday the 28th January. They noticed that there was no flag flying from the Palace mast. They were two days too late. Khartoum had fallen and Gordon was dead.

CHAPTER TEN

Everyone here is staggered with the news about Khartoum" Brocklehurst wrote to Louie on the 8th February from Korti. "Too late again, just as one was going to shake hands with him, as it seemed. Wolseley has got carte blanche we hear, to do what he likes, but what that will be goodness only knows. It is a curious thing that the natives here will not believe that Khartoum has fallen and somehow I half hope that there may have been some hideous mistake and that Gordon will turn up and things come right yet.

You may imagine things are not very merry here - astounding rumours flying about and everyone with a long face, asking for news. It is bad enough here at the end of a telegraph, but it must be much worse with the advance columns.

If Gordon is dead, it is only our loss as he always said remember when I am dead not to be sorry as death is what I have longed for all my life. But I cannot realise that he is dead. I rode into the desert at daybreak this morning and felt very gloomy, but God is good....."

Back in England the news of the fall of Khartoum and Gordon's death shocked and distressed the British people. None more so than Queen Victoria, who wrote to Gordon's sister, Augusta, "that the promises of support were not fulfilled - which I so frequently and so constantly pressed on those who asked him to go - is to me grief inexpressible."

Meanwhile the whole of Britain went into "unofficial mourning of extraordinary intensity" and this was echoed in countries throughout the world where people had been anxiously following the course of the siege and praying that Gordon could hold out. Philip Magnus in his book on Kitchener described "a mood of hysteria which lasted about three weeks drew crowds every day to Downing Street in the hope that they might have a chance to hoot and jeer at the Prime Minister." And the same night that Wolseley finally wired to London his conviction that Gordon was dead Gladstone was booed by an angry London crowd as he rather unfeelingly went to a performance at the Criterion Theatre.

Back in the desert Gordon's last letter to Brocklehurst [see page 90] had turned up, together with the rest of those included in the "Last Despatch" which were found by Sir Charles Wilson in the steamer *Bourdein* at Shendy. Brocklehurst immediately sent it through to Louie. "You will also find enclosed a tiny photograph of my letter to him by Curtis (so Curtis got his letters thro'). One volume of Gordon's Diary, the last from November 5 to December 16, Sir C Wilson brought back here - the others are too bulky and are coming on later with all the telegrams which passed between Gordon and Baring, which Gordon also had sent to the steamer in a box - they will be uncomfortable news for Baring.

Wolseley let me read the Diary on condition I would say nothing about it (by the way he also asked me not to publish in newspapers my own letter when he gave it to me and I promised I would not - so you mustn't). The Diary is most interesting and full of bits of fun. Of course it will be a facer for the Government if published and they will try to suppress it - pigeon hole it.

But it must be published. It does not belong to the Government but to Gordon's family, who should publish it just as it is, no pruning.

A man has arrived here from Khartoum who says he saw Gordon shot and saw our steamer come up to Khartoum. Sir C Wilson says he must certainly have been an eye witness of the steamer advance, so I fear his story is true. Yes, I am afraid almost too certainly my old man is dead because we were 48 hours 2880 minutes too late. Such is life my dear wife, and its no use regretting this and that, as Wolseley said to me, 'There's only one thing to do, look present facts in the face and laugh at them'

Write to the people mentioned in Gordon's letter and give his message, particularly to the MBs, also to the Baroness [Baroness Burdett-Coutts] to say that Curtis got his letters thro'. Curtis is now at Metemmeh and keeps writing to me. It will be a great blow to him as I had promised to get him employment under Gordon.

I expect we shall be here some time now, but you will know all this in England better than I do. If we stay here this summer and I can send for you I will".

There were many versions of how Gordon was killed - some said he defended himself and fought his way down into the Palace garden before he was overwhelmed. It seems likely that in the terrible carnage of that January morning he was speared to death rather than shot. One version was that Gordon had shut himself up in a room for two days and killed everyone who came near him until his ammunition was gone when he himself was killed, sword in hand. We do know that his head was cut off and taken to Omdurman to be displayed before the Mahdi who, it is rumoured was disappointed by Gordon's death. He had specifically ordered that Gordon was to be kept alive. He had hoped to imprison him and convert him to the true faith. One account even claimed that this had happened and he had turned Mussulman.

"Gordon I am afraid is dead, though I can't realize it yet and I do so want to see him again", Brocklehurst wrote to Louie.

"I am so glad that people do appreciate him at last all round. What a sermon his life is - it makes a man of one to think of him.....However his tragical death seems to be having an effect in England which perhaps his life could not have, and the study of his life may cause mighty changes in England, which I take it are wanted. Gladstone and his Cabinet are being blamed for this business, yet I cannot see that they are more to blame than those who keep them in power. If England as a nation, or the bulk of Englishmen, in their hankering after other men's goods are content to keep in power men who pander to that vice regardless of our vast Imperial responsibilities, then England will soon cease to be an Empire by the will of the majority. Perhaps a healthier political life may spring up from the study of the story of Charles George Gordon?

I could find it in my heart to abuse Gladstone, Baring and the rest, but somehow the story of the woman taken in adultery prevents me. If only those who are perfect cast stones, there will be no stone throwing, what do you think? It seems to me we have to act on our own little part as best we can, but we must in no wise set ourselves up as judges."

Gordon himself could not have expressed it better and this showed how influenced Brocklehurst had been by his mentor.

What is more surprising is to discover that Brocklehurst, who had been born into one of the most Radical families in the North of England, had apparently turned Tory and imperialist.

As he tried to come to terms with Gordon's death the expedition force was moving back down the Nile. Wolseley, devastated by the failure of his relief expedition and the death of his old comrade, wanted to advance on Berber and build up his force for a counter attack on the Mahdi in the Autumn.

As a result the base at Korti, where Brocklehurst was stationed, was soon very busy, as both columns moved back - "The outlook here is very gloomy, the force retreating back here for summer quarters. I suppose we shall make a job of it in the Autumn, but if Gordon is dead there is no curing that and it will be dreary work. From all accounts we shall be well roasted as well."

"The place is swarming again with soldiers and sailors, camels, horses, donkeys, Arabs, Negroes, Aden boys - all colours, shapes and sizes - a very lively scene", he described it to Aunt Emma."The soldiers (those that are not ill) seem very well, but are mostly in rags, as you may imagine. The saddest thing of all is when a convoy of wounded comes in from the desert - some of them poor things having come all the way from Metemmeh. They are carried in two ways - the best cases on camels - 2 men on a camel in sort of panniers (stretchers fastened to the camel saddle one on each side) and the worst cases on stretchers, carried by a native.

A sight of this sort rather discounts the Glory of War, but as old Palmerston said 'Man is a quarrelsome beast and always will be' so if it's a necessity it's a good job it is considered 'glorious'.

Two hundred also of Gordon's men (those found on the steamer) came in. A very curious weird scene, some walking, some on camels, some wounded, all armed and all cheery - a wild ragged looking lot. Two of them are now in my lines. They talk so much of him and say nothing could have beaten him but treachery. I gave them a sheep to comfort their poor tummicks for they looked very starved, but they are in good hands as one of them is a friend of my stud groom - a gigantic black than whom there is no kinder old party.

I think we shall have trouble with the Arabs here as they are not so friendly since the news of Khartoum and I think will all disappear into the desert again to wait and see which way the cat jumps. Our retreat back from Metemmeh is having a bad effect."

The desert also was at its most inhospitable - "awful dust storms, living in fact in an atmosphere like a bad bit of the Ascot road in race week on a hot day - everything smothered in dust, one has to keep blowing it off the paper as one writes-very hot as well (105 in the shade they say in middle day). ....perspiring , with barely enough clothes on for decency and sitting in a draught. The tents are double but the sun comes thro' so hot one has to keep a hat on. ...the flies also keep one in a ferment. Yesterday we started sand flies, a sort of big midge that stings - they are bad and I trust will not continue.

"No-one here can make out what is going to happen, but it is the general feeling in camp that we shall not stay here this summer (the wish being father to the thought I take it)", he told Louie, who was very anxious to come and join him in the Sudan. His next posting was to be Abu Fatmeh - 10 days by camel from Wady Halfa and there was no way she would be allowed to make the journey, "but I do hope to be with you, somehow, somewhere soon", he reassured her.

The box of swords which Gordon had sent to Brocklehurst with the last despatch had been found - empty, of course - and

Curtis had brought back some of the leaden medals which Gordon had struck for his men in Khartoum - 'Siege of Khartoum' is written on them in Arabic. Brocklehurst sent four of them to his brother Harry with instructions to send one each to Baroness Coutts, P. Ralli and their Aunt Emma Dent. She added hers to the small museum she was making in her home at Sudeley Castle and when it was later displayed there she noted that Gordon's medals had become highly sought after, and in many instances even an offer of their weight in gold failed to induce the lucky owners to part with them. Brocklehurst also offered to send her one of the longboots worn by Burnaby when he was killed in the battle at Abu Klea, which were curiosities because of their great size.

Curtis, after all his adventures, came to an untimely end when, returning to Cairo with the money he had made from acting as a contractor and interpreter to the Army, he was set upon , robbed and murdered on a lonely road near Sarras by his native bearers. His body was never found but his servants were recognised and seized at some considerable distance up the river.

I have not been able to discover who P. Ralli was, except that he was one of the group who communicated with Gordon through Curtis. and he now writes to Brocklehurst asking if he can help him in recovering Stewart's diary. The Government he felt would not be keen - "they have enough on their hands with Gordon's which I think they wish was in the lowest depth of the Nile: they now say that he tells them in it to prune before publication, this means that all the interesting facts will be cut out.

I can't help smiling at reading the supposed preparation for an autumn campaign" Ralli wrote.

"You will be no more allowed to go to Khartoum than I will be Prime Minister next week and all the references to Berber etc. etc. are humbug. The state of things here is very funny, as the Govt, being at hopeless loggerheads with one another, want to be turned out, and the Tories being also at loggerheads, are trembling lest a snap vote (which may come off at any moment) should put them into office: between the two our affairs do not prosper.

This letter is, of course, between ourselves as you may not like in your official capacity to take any private steps about Stewart's papers". He suggested that Brocklehurst might perhaps talk to Kitchener about it - "he knows these precious scoundrels in the Soudan better than most people."

[Henry Keown-Boyd has since told me that P.Ralli is almost certainly Pandeli Ralli who was a friend of Kitchener. The Rallis were (and are) an Anglo-Greek family who made fortunes in India and Egypt.]

We don't know whether Brocklehurst was able to take any action over this, because by now he was on the march again - this time to Abu Fatmeh - 150 miles north of Korti where there was supposed to be plenty of camel grazing- 'it would make you shudder to see a camel eat thorns' he said. He had been very distressed by the hundreds which had already died in the desert after not having been fed for five days or watered for seven days during the fighting.

"My charges are in a pitiful state, food for them is very scarce and it's a struggle to get anything to put in their poor tummicks....which are now quite concave" He had grown fond of the "extraordinary beasts who work on with their backs not just sore but in a state past description, apparently not minding. (20 miles a day with 400lbs we consider easy marching). They will also take any number of bullets without flinching. A good camel is a very pleasant thing to ride and a bad one is very much the reverse."

"Last night I heard a mysterious noise just outside my tent - Robbers said I, but on poking my head out I found it was a camel that had got loose and come and snuggled himself down right up against my tent door - my head nearly ran against his, but he did not seem a bit disconcerted and went on chewing the cud and looked at me as much as to say, all right old chap, go to bed again it's only me. He looked so comfy I could not send him back to his line, so I left him, which generosity he repaid by eating my straw carpet, much to Crowe's indignation in the morning."

At Abul Fatmeh Brocklehurst was at last going to be free of tent living as he had taken a house - or rather a location on the river. "There is no house at present but there is a temple thereabouts, which if in any way adjacent I shall try and rig up into one - regardless of archaeologists."

By April the British Government faced with another possible war in Afghanistan ordered Wolseley and his force to return from the Sudan. The ever-persistent Louie succeeded in getting out to Cairo and she and Brocklehurst were happily reunited there in May.

"I am thankful to say I have got my John back and he is looking wonderfully well" she wrote to Aunt Emma from Shepheards Hotel. "He arrived on Wednesday last having had a very slow journey from Assouan in consequence of the river [Nile] being so low. In fact they spent most of the time sticking on various sandbanks.

It is such a comfort to have the old thing here! Now our only anxiety is to get definite orders for him to go home, but up to now his original orders (which were to return to Dongola when he had paid and dismissed the 200 Aden camel drivers he brought down) have not been cancelled. Sir R Buller telegraphed to Ld Wolseley about him some days ago, but he has had no answer.

Unfortunately he left Dongola before the abandonment of Soudan was announced and the Remount Depot was still in working order - so that there is a good deal still to be done in the way of settling and paying up accounts, but I do hope they will get someone there to do it if possible.

I am afraid I shall have to go home without him if he has to remain any time as I don't stand the heat very well. It is pretty bad - the worst day has been 107 in the shade - today is a trifle cooler I think.

I hear today that the return of the Guards to England is countermanded and they are to remain at Alexandria. I don't like the news at all. I am so afraid we shall not be able to avoid war with Russia."

In fact Brocklehurst was back in London by July, when he wrote to reassure Aunt Emma that his campaign accounts had passed the General 'with flying colours'. During the campaign he had been mentioned in dispatches and on his return was promoted to brevet Major.

On the 15th February Lord Wolseley had written to the Prince of Wales from Camp Korti:

"I always like to tell Your Royal Highness of the men in the Household cavalry who have done remarkably well. First comes Regy Talbot...Then there is Brocklehurst, a first rate officer & Lord Cochrane & Sir J Willoughby. We have no more earnest officers in the Army than they are."

As far as the British Government was concerned the Sudan had now been evacuated and deserted. The Mahdi, flushed with the success of his conquest, did not wait for the afterlife to enjoy the promised sensual pleasures. He grew fat and prosperous in Omdurman and died there on the 22nd June 1885 - having survived Gordon by only five months -reputedly having been poisoned by an outraged virgin. Abdulla Ibn Sayed Muhammad was nominated the First Khalifa (successor) to the Mahdi and continued to fight the Islamic cause.

It was 1896 before Kitchener, who was now Sirdar (commander-in-chief of the Egyptian army), undertook the reconquest of the Sudan. Brocklehurst was not among the British officers who joined his force, perhaps because it is said Kitchener did not want officers who were married.

By September 1898 Kitchener commanded a force of 20,000 and was ready to attack. His offensive culminated in the Battle of Omdurman, when at dawn on the morning of the 2nd September 1898, 2,500 Arabs met the cavalry charge of the 21st Lancers and the British artillery fire - "No white troops would have faced that torrent of death for five minutes. It was not a battle but an execution", said one observer. The official figures for the appalling slaughter counted nearly 11,000 Sudanese killed, 16,000 wounded and 4,000 prisoners. Total casualties among Kitchener's regiments - 48 killed and 428 wounded.

There was a strong element of revenge in that final battle and the memorial service for Gordon which the triumphant British force held afterwards in Khartoum. "Surely he is avenged", Queen Victoria wrote. None of them seemed to realise that Gordon would not have courted or believed in revenge. His satisfaction would come later from the Gordon College which was founded in Khartoum when the city was rebuilt - now the University of the Sudan - and the Gordon

School in Woking, our living National Memorial to General Gordon.

G.W. Steevens - the newspaper man who went with Kitchener to Khartoum wrote later in his book of that title.

'With Maxim-Nordenfeldt and Bible we buried Gordon after the manner of his race. The parade was over, the troops dismissed and for a short space we walked in Gordon's garden. Gordon has become a legend with his countrymen and they all but deify him dead who would never have heard of him had he lived. But in the garden you somehow come to know Gordon the man, not the myth, and to feel near him. Here was an Englishman doing his duty alone and at the instant peril of his life; yet he loved his garden.'

It was 22 years after Gordon's death that Baring, by then Lord Cromer, became the first to detract from the Gordon legend in his book *'Modern Egypt'*. and in particular to blame the British press for their interference. WT Stead was incensed and wrote to Brocklehurst in fury that "a man convicted out of his own mouth of a persistent policy of procedural interference which cost Gordon his life.....should have put so cruel a libel upon the memory of the dead."

Brocklehurst, who was in Egypt at the time, wrote to assure Stead of his support. "I always felt Cromer would do this, and now he has done it and it's for us to prove him wrong. Tout comprendre, c'est tout pardonner has always been my favourite saying, in which I absolutely believe, so I've got to stick to it now, sick as I feel. One must realise that Lord Cromer, with all his brains, is of the earth earthy, and Gordon to him was a lunatic, no more, no less".

If Cromer had understood Gordon Brocklehurst contended there would have been no heroic sacrifice at Khartoum to teach the world that Christ was still a living force. There was comfort at least in that reflection - "Think of the loss to this poor old weary world."

CHAPTER ELEVEN

Queen Victoria was already beginning to notice John Brocklehurst. "His Colonel told me the other day that he was dining with the Queen and she asked him a great deal about John" Louie wrote to Aunt Emma. "She said she took such an interest in him and was so glad to have the opportunity of saying what a promising, gallant young officer she thought him and how proud she was of him". However it was to be another fourteen years before the Queen could find room for him in her household.

In the meantime while John Brocklehurst had been in the desert some changes had taken place in the family. In March 1885 John Coucher Dent, Aunt Emma's husband, died and left the Dent family home, Sudeley Castle and its estate to Brocklehurst's younger brother Harry.

This came about because John and Emma Dent had no children and when John Coucher Dent began considering the inheritance of the Castle he believed that he had no blood relations who should succeed him. In the event he had overlooked some members of his mother's family the de Merics who might have been considered his lawful heirs.

He was also apparently unaware of an illegitimate brother,

Mark, who had been born to his parents, Thomas and Mary Dent, four years before their marriage. This birth was kept secret because his mother, Mary Coucher was only a girl of fifteen at the time. The families, who were well known and respected in the neighbourhood, arranged for the birth to be hushed up and the baby to be adopted by Thomas's cousin, Mark Dent. Four years later Thomas and Mary were married and produced two legitimate sons - John Coucher Dent and his brother Martin, who died before him. The love-child Mark Dent was never acknowledged by the family and when he grew up emigrated to Australia and latterly to New Zealand.

There is no indication that John Coucher Dent ever knew of Mark's existence and in 1881, when he made his will, his concern was for the continuation of the Dent name, threatened with dying out, and the guardianship of Sudeley Castle by someone who would live there and care for it as their principal home. He and Emma decided that the Castle would be safe in the hands of one of her nephews, particularly her brother Henry's orphaned sons.

As the first born and Emma's favourite John Brocklehurst might have been expected to inherit, but John Coucher Dent considered him rather a 'flash harry' and had never cared for 'his grand and dashing style' this, coupled with the fact that he and Louie had no children, meant that he was passed over for Harry, one of his younger brothers..

John Coucher Dent made his intentions clear in the letter to Emma dated 1881 which accompanied his will. 'JFB has at present no children. HDB is going to be married - one could think he is likely to have some'. John wrote. It was also fortuitous that Harry had been christened Henry Dent Brocklehurst and therefore already carried the Dent name. And a year later, in 1882, his first son was born, ensuring John Coucher Dent's wish for a family succession to the Castle which has continued through to the current owners of Sudeley.

There is no suggestion that John Brocklehurst resented losing the chance to own the Castle, even though by this time Harry had almost an embarrassment of land, as his wife, Marion, had recently inherited Middlethorpe Manor in Yorkshire, on the death of her father the Hon Egremont Lascelles. The brothers had always been good friends and particularly used to enjoy the summer race meetings at Newmarket when they would invariably send their hacks down to the course and watch the racing from the saddle - 'it was delightful to see the brothers cantering along the July course indistinguishable for the ease and grace of their finished horsemanship', said one observer.

Johnny was also now established in his Army career and well on the way to take command of his regiment. Harry had always taken a more relaxed view of soldiering, particularly once he had transferred from the 5th Lancers to the Second Life Guards. "Harry says he was galloping orderly the other day - didn't wait long enough to hear the General's order and so gave it wrong and caught it hot in not parliamentary language and as there were 90 guns out he made a fine mess", his Aunt Emma recorded in her diary. "However the General has asked him since to a ball and made it up".

Johnny and Louie had a town house in Mount Street but in 1893 decided to sell 'The Willows,' their house on the banks of the Thames at Windsor and build themselves a country house in the great hunting shires - 'there is no better known figure than his in the hunting field - always admirably mounted, his weight carries him well to the fore" Bailey's Magazine reported of Brocklehurst. He needed space in which to breed and enjoy horses for according to Bailey's he was recognised as "one of the best judges of a horse in England and has also a deserved reputation as a horseman; few can equal him in kind and judicious handling of a high-spirited young one He has never registered colours, but for some years past has kept a few good brood mares and he has bred some good stock from them."

As well as the the hunting he and Louie had many friends with houses in the Leicestershire and Rutland countryside and his younger brother Alfred, who had married General Little's daughter, Florence was now at Melton Mowbray. Brocklehurst bought a couple of hundred acres at Langham under the shadow of the gorse-covered Ranksborough Hill, known in hunting circles as 'a sure find', and built a solid and unpretentious house there, soon filling the surrounding meadows with his horses and cattle herds.

His army duties continued to be dominated by ceremonies. In December 1887, following the Queen's Golden Jubilee, Aunt Emma recorded in her diary: 'The Queen had a great reception when she arrived at Windsor and her statue was uncovered. Johnny and soldiers were keeping the streets and when that was over he had to take a troop down to Eton to escort 900 Etonians up to the Castle where they lit torches and lanterns - marched round the quadrangle and sang songs etc. "It was" writes Louie "a very pretty sight". Johnny very busy afterwards doing escort duty for diverse Kings and Queens.

'In the winter he and Louie went to Paris to work up his French and then to visit his old friends Lord and Lady Vivian in Brussels. [Lord Vivian who was now the Minister there had been the British Consul-General in Alexandria when Brocklehurst first met Gordon in Egypt in 1877].

Brussels was very gay now in the season and Johnny had dined with King Leopold.'

In 1895 he took command of his regiment, the Blues, and according to 'The World' 'has his regiment in splendid order, as is perhaps only to be expected considering the great interest he has ever taken in his profession and the good material with which he has to work He is a good all-round man with plenty of professional enthusiasm, a commanding and soldier-like presence, charm of manner and considerable force of character.'.

A year earlier the Duke of Cambridge, the Queen's cousin, who had been Commander-in-Chief of the Horse Guards for nearly 40 years finally resigned. For some time he had been resisting Lord Wolseley's attempts to press for army reform. The Duke insisted that he was not against change, but that change must come when it could no longer be avoided. His priorities were ceremonial parades, set field days and fine uniforms, and he believed that promotion should only be by seniority and long service.

The contrast between him and Wolseley , the famous fighting general, could not have been more extreme. Wolseley, who had been battle hardened in his twenties. and lost the sight of his right eye while being struck by a bursting shell in the Crimea, said the Duke "knows as much of modern warfare - indeed of any warfare - as my top boot does." The Duke, in his turn, regarded Wolseley as a "desperate reformer", for his proposals, which included short service commissions and promotion on merit. He made every attempt to block Wolseley's progress and in 1880 had suggested that the Prince of Wales, who was his friend and ally, should be made Colonel-in-Chief of the Household Cavalry and support him against his vociferous army critic.This worked well in the Duke's favour, and he was able to prevent Wolseley getting his peerage, and a voice in the House of Lords, until after his victory in the Egyptian War in 1882.

However, after the Prince of Wales had persuaded the Duke of Cambridge, who was then aged 76, to resign, he tried to manoeuvre for the Duke of Connaught (Queen Victoria's favourite son) to succeed him as Commander-in-Chief by giving Wolseley the Berlin Embassy. Although the Kaiser had expressed delight at the prospect of Wolseley as Ambassador the scheme misfired when Wolseley was invited by the Cabinet to choose between Berlin and the Horse Guards and, as would be expected, he chose the latter.

Brocklehurst was delighted when Wolseley was made Colonel-in-Chief of his regiment the Blues and Wolseley responded to his enthusiastic welcome with a letter saying 'I have been at times tempted with offers of Regiments of Life Guards and Foot Guards but always answered that I would wait for the Blues in the hope that the Queen would give them to me. She has done so and I feel sincerely proud of having my name thus associated with a Regiment that I had always considered the first of all Regiments in Europe.

Believe me also when I tell you that I value this honour all the more because it once again brings me into touch with a Commanding Officer whom I learned to value and esteem ten years ago when in the deserts of the Nile.'

The year of Queen Victoria's Diamond Jubilee, 1897, was a time for much more ceremonial for the Blues and amid the general rejoicing the only sour note Brocklehurst recorded was sounded by his friend the journalist WT Stead.

Stead and Brocklehurst had remained in touch since Stead's interview with Gordon in 1884, after which Stead had continued his campaigning journalism in the *Pall Mall Gazette*, most sensationally in his exposure of the Victorian sex trade in child prostitution *"The Maiden Tribute to Modern Babylon"*, which led not only to his being sent to gaol for three months, but also to a change in the legal age of consent.

At the Jubilee his target was the Prince of Wales. Having watched the Prince walk down Westminster Abbey beside his brother-in-law. the Kaiser and noted the contrast between the rather dumpy figure of the Prince and the more distinguished bearing of the Emperor. Stead wrote a leader in the *Pall Mall Gazette* giving an unfavourable comparison between the "fat little man in red who cut so poor a figure beside his brother-in-law in white". This caused a row, as might be expected, and earned the following rebuke from Brocklehurst.

'If the Prince of Wales, wishing to speak ill of the Editor of the *Pall Mall Gazette* prefaced his remarks by saying "That gaunt wild-looking individual, always badly dressed" would it not appear to you pointless bad taste, taking away to a great extent the value of any further remarks he had to make on the subject?'

In a friendly note, written a week later Brocklehurst added 'You are not a small man, so don't do small things'.

The turn of the century was saddened for him by the deaths of his two Brocklehurst aunts, Marianne and Emma, who had, particularly since the death of his parents, played such an important part in his life.

Aunt Marianne, who had first introduced him to Gordon, had continued her interest in the Arabian deserts and become a recognised Egyptologist. Her sister, Emma, had tried to persuade Marianne to give her collection of Egyptian treasures to boost the museum she had created at Sudeley Castle, but

Marianne felt that they should remain in Macclesfield and in 1898 she created a Museum in West Park, Macclesfield for the purpose, which was endowed by their brother, Peter. Apart from this main interest, she enjoyed the small farm which she and her partner Mary Booth ran at their home the Bagstones on her younger brother Philip's Swythamley estate; was a keen sportswoman, an expert fly fisher and capital shot, so it seemed almost inexplicable that in October 1898 she should fall into what was described as 'severe melancholia' and take her own life. The Brocklehursts succeeded in keeping secret the reason for her sudden death, so that she could have a Christian burial in the churchyard at Wincle.

Aunt Emma, whose generous annual allowance to Johnny Brocklehurst had helped him to meet the expensive life style of a cavalry officer, died in 1900, leaving Sudeley Castle vacant for Harry and his family, but not before she had learnt with pride that Johnny had joined the Royal household as Equerry to Queen Victoria..

Her last news of him was that he was holed up in Ladysmith where he was in command of the cavalry and that Queen Victoria was enquiring anxiously for his safety.

CHAPTER TWELVE

On the 5th July 1899 Queen Victoria recorded in her journal that Colonel Brocklehurst dined with her at Windsor. "I had already seen the latter in the afternoon & am appointing him as Equerry in the place of poor Ld Strafford. He is very tall & soldierlike looking, between 40 & 50, & has been 25 years in the Blues, the command of which he is just giving up."

We know that the Queen had been interested in Brocklehurst for some time and the death of Lord Strafford provided the first opportunity for him to join the Royal household. Major-General Sir Henry Ewart wrote to him in May warning him that the appointment was about to be made, but that the Queen 'wishes nothing to be mentioned for some days'. This was followed by an official letter from the Keeper of the Privy Purse, Lt-Col.Sir Fleetwood Edwards at Balmoral saying 'The Queen is very pleased that you accept the post of Equerry that she has offered you. By H M's commands I am asking Ewart to gazette the appointment when a month has elapsed since Strafford's death."

His congratulations on the appointment were followed by another letter from Major-General Sir Henry Ewart chiding Brocklehurst for his standing on ceremony with 'Don't you think that after all these years you might dispense with the

"General" formality.? You will not serve in future under anybody except the Queen and you will find her, as I do, the best of mistresses. I am so glad you have accepted. I enclose you a note from the Queen....the questions which you can answer to me are of no great importance'. These were inquiries whether Brocklehurst spoke French and whether his father was still alive.

Brocklehurst kept the hand-written note from the Queen among his treasured records even though Ewart had asked him to return it. Queen Victoria disliked typewriters and insisted that even her official correspondence should be conducted in writing. As her sight began to fail, her Private Secretary, Sir Arthur Bigge changed his handwriting to a fine script and used ink which was as thick and black as pitch, inventing a heated tray on which he could dry the letters before submitting them to the Queen for signature.

Brocklehurst's appointment was greeted with some astonishment in the press and in court circles. At the time it was very unusual for anyone outside the aristocracy to be appointed to the Royal household. He had never seemed to be particularly ambitious, but his courtesy and charm, together with the simple-minded integrity which had so endeared him to Gordon, had brought him a long way from the family mills of Macclesfield and Todmorden to be given a place at court. The post of Equerry-in-ordinary held a very close relationship with the Sovereign and then commanded a salary of £600 a year. "Some of the handsomest and most gallant of soldiers have been her [Queen Victoria's]equerries" commented *The World*, and now "Brocklehurst, the *beau sabreur* - a giant in inches, a child in simple-minded religion, the staunch friend and disciple of Charles Gordon."

However he had hardly had time to take up his appointment, when in August 1899, Lord Wolseley, who was now Commander-in-Chief of the Army, wrote to Queen Victoria asking for Brocklehurst to serve as his ADC.

'Lord Wolseley is aware that Her Majesty has recently appointed that officer to be one of the Queen's Equerries, but his being A.D.C to the Comndr in Chief would not in any ways whatever interfere with his duties as Equerry' he maintained. 'Colonel Brocklehurst is an excellent officer, & one of the best Colonels in Her Majesty's Cavalry.'

Queen Victoria asked the Prince of Wales's opinion 'It is of course a new departure.' To which he replied 'Much surprised. Consider it impossible. As he is Queen's Equerry his duties must clash'. Sir Arthur Bigge sent the following tactful letter to Wolseley:

'The Queen after careful consideration is inclined to think that as Colonel Brocklehurst has been already appointed one of Her Majesty's Equerries, to now make him your Aide-de-Camp would not only be a departure from precedent but would probably lead to difficulties in the proper fulfilment of the duties of both offices. Sir John McNeill, when A.D.C. to the Duke of Cambridge was obliged to resign that position when appointed Equerry to the Queen.

Under these circumstances HM feels that it would be advisable not to make the proposed submission. It is however a great satisfaction to The Queen to think that Her selection of Colonel Brocklehurst has been so fully endorsed by the Commander-in-Chief in thus wishing to have the services of that officer on his Staff.'

This would have been the end of this particular tug-of-war if events in South Africa had not demanded Brocklehurst's return to the Army.

The discoveries of gold and diamonds in the Transvaal, and moves by Cecil Rhodes to take control of South Africa, had led to conflict with the Boers - the descendants of the Dutch settlers who had first set up a trading station at the Cape of Good Hope in 1652. During the Napoleonic Wars Britain, recognising the significance of the Cape as a naval base on the sea route to India and the East, had taken permanent possession of the colony, until, in the 1830's the Afrikaaners, finding their basic tenets threatened by the British emancipation of slavery, undertook a mass exodus of some 10,000 people - The Great Trek - from the Cape Colony across the Orange and Vaal Rivers to found two new independent Boer republics - the Transvaal and the Orange Free State.

However, once gold was discovered in the Transvaal, Britain acted swiftly to annexe the republic. This was reversed in 1881 after the leader of the Boers, Paul Kruger, led a rebellion (the lst Boer War) which resulted in the British defeat at Majuba.

Transvaal's independence was restored, but the influx of 'Uitlanders' (foreign outsiders) who had swarmed into the area in the gold rush began to threaten the Boers' way of life and Paul Kruger, as President of the republic, resisted their demands for political rights.

As a result of this, in December 1895 Cecil Rhodes, then Prime Minister of the Cape, tried to engineer an uprising of the Uitlanders in Johannesburg which would be re-inforced by a flying column of Cape Chartered Company troops under the command of his friend Dr Leander Jameson.

The 'Jameson Raid' as it became known, was a terrible failure. Jameson, who had moved in too fast, had to be disowned; the Uitlanders did not rebel and Rhodes had to resign as Prime Minister of the Cape, while the Kaiser cabled his congratulations to Kruger on putting down the raid. We will learn later of Brocklehurst's friendship with Rhodes and the part he played in the political aftermath of the Raid.

In his continuing efforts to stop a further war, in 1897 Joseph Chamberlain, the Secretary of State for the Colonies appointed Sir Alfred Milner as High Commissioner in South Africa. A journalist, Milner had been deputy editor to WT Stead on the *Pall Mall Gazette* and at first it seemed that he would be prepared to build a partnership with the Boers. But he soon came to distrust them and by the following year, 1898, he was convinced that only a show of force would break their intransigence.

The British press, with the exception of the *Pall Mall Gazette,* took an anti-Kruger line and with Chamberlain admitting that Kruger would 'bluff up to the cannon's mouth' the decision was taken for a show of force. Wolseley mobilised the whole of General Sir Redvers Buller's 1st Army Corps and a cavalry division of about 35,000 troops. Buller, who knew the Boers better than any other general, having fought in the Zulu Wars and the 1st Boer War, did not regard them as a serious military adversary. 'They were used to fighting Kaffirs', he declared. 'The British could beat them easily'.

Lieutenant-General Sir George White was selected as general in command of the extra force and chose for his staff Colonels Ian Hamilton and Sir Henry Rawlinson.

At that time the generals in the Army were split into two rival rings - Wolseley's 'Africans' who had fought with him in Egypt and the Sudan and Roberts' 'Indians', veterans of the Indian and Afghan frontier wars. Lord Roberts had narrowly missed command in the 1st Boer War and he and Wolseley were implacable adversaries. White's choice of two of Roberts' keenest partisans needed balancing with someone from the Wolseley camp and Buller proposed Brocklehurst. To lure him back from the Royal household he was to be offered, and accepted, the command of a brigade of cavalry in Natal with the rank of Major-General, to become, aged 47, the youngest General officer at the front.

In telegraphing Queen Victoria's consent to Brocklehurst's appointment Sir Arthur Bigge wrote, 'HM was loth to let you go as she feels you will be so valuable to her as an equerry. But I promised that the war would not last more than 3 or 4 months and that you would probably only miss your November and February waits. I am so glad for your sake that you have got the commission and sincerely wish you good luck.'

Once again critical voices were raised at Brocklehurst's selection, with the suggestion that he had only been chosen to accompany Sir George White because of his Royal connections. This was quickly refuted in the press with the following: "Sir Redvers Buller has had a voice in all the appointments in South Africa. It was he who so strongly urged the appointment of General Brocklehurst of the Blues to command a cavalry brigade in Natal. Brocklehurst's worth was instilled into Buller by General French who has formed a deliberate opinion that Brocklehurst is one of the best of our modern cavalry officers. All this is worth emphasising, for the outside general public were inclined to believe that the appointment was due to Court influence, General Brocklehurst having lately been made an equerry to the Queen."

This view of Brocklehurst's worth as a cavalry commander was not shared by Lieutenant- Colonel Sir Henry Rawlinson, with whom he was later to be 'holed up' in Ladysmith. Dismissing Brocklehurst as one of the red-tabbed officers of the old school and saying he was 'known ironically as Poglehurst' he claimed he had 'neither the dash nor the brains to command cavalry'. His opinion is not borne out by any of the accounts of action in South Africa but is unfortunately quoted in Thomas Pakenham's book *The Boer War* which has given it some prominence.

Brocklehurst was known in the army as 'Brock' or 'Big Brock' and probably nicknamed 'Poglehurst' by Rawlinson and his friends, whose disparagement of him may have had more to do with the rivalry between the Wolseley and Roberts rings in the army than with Brocklehurst's own supposed deficiencies. He certainly was not the bumbling idiot depicted by Rawlinson.

However, all this was to come as Brocklehurst set sail on *The Mexican* for Durban. On the 11th October 1899 the Boers had declared war.

CHAPTER THIRTEEN

They said that the war would be over by Christmas. Instead Brocklehurst spent Christmas trapped in Ladysmith with the rest of Sir George White's 13,000 men, - where they were forced to eat their horses - and the main enemies were fatigue and disease rather than the surrounding Boers.

The conflict had started badly. The Boers heavily outnumbered the British advance force - they also had the advantage of being familiar with the country, were excellent rifle shots and their Krupps long range guns proved superior to the British armaments

Although Buller had impressed on White that he should not push too far forward into Natal but stay on the defensive behind the Tegela River and prepare the way for the main invasion force, White decided to press on and garrison Ladysmith, which with its railway junction would make an excellent supply base. This proved to be a terrible mistake. By the time he reached the town the Boers were already advancing from the North of Natal and had cut off the water supply. However, armed with 20 squadrons and eleven batteries, White declared positively "By tomorrow night there will not be a Boer within 20 miles of Ladysmith." As it was by the evening of

October 30th the whole of White's 13,000 command had been flung back into the town with 300 men killed and wounded and nearly 1,000 prisoners.

Brocklehurst had been with General French when the cavalry made a dawn attack on the Boer force at Elandslaagte on the line of communication between Ladysmith and Dundee, but even they ended up at Ladysmith in some disarray. Two days later the Boers cut the railway line and at 2.30pm on October 30th the siege of Ladysmith had begun. Kimberley on the northernmost border of the Orange Free State was also besieged as was Mafeking.

Ladysmith was described by Winston Churchill, who was a newspaper correspondent in South Africa during the war, as a 'regular trap'. 'The town and cantonment stand in a huge circle of hills which enclamp it on all sides like the arms of a giant and though so great is the circle that only guns of the heavier class can reach the town from the heights, once an enemy has established itself on those heights it is beyond the power of the garrison to dislodge him, or perhaps even break out.'

White decided to deploy his cavalry to make some sorties outside the town and on the 6th November *The Times* carried the headline: 'General Brocklehurst successfully encounters the enemy.' 'General Brocklehurst taking the 18th and 19th Hussars with Volunteer Cavalry and one battery of Mounted Infantry operated against a reported movement of the enemy on the Maritzburg road' read their correspondent's report. 'He found the enemy with guns in laager in force at midday. General Brocklehurst reinforced by the 5th Dragoons, Royston's Horse and two batteries drove the enemy from his position, shelled 3 guns into silence and headed 1,000 Boers from the Maritzburg Road. The Imperial Light Horse passsed too far into the gulley and were extricated by the 5th Dragoons. All got back safely under heavy fire'.

Queen Victoria recording news of the war in her journal wrote:

6 November "....Heard that a message from Ladysmith by carrier pigeon had been received dated the 3rd to the effect that on the previous day Col.Brocklehurst [General was only his field rank] with Cavalry & Field Batteries had effectively shelled Boer laager without loss on our side....On the 3rd Col. Brocklehurst with Cavalry & Artillery engaged the enemy to the southwest of Ladysmith, fighting lasting several hours. Our losses small. Troops in good health & spirits, wounded doing well - This is much more satisfactory."

On the 7th November the Queen wrote "...After tea received further news from S.Africa confirming the good reports we had had in the morning from Reuter. There have been no hostilities since the 3rd. During that day's bombardment, heavy shells fell into the Hospital, but injured no one. The troops under Col: Brocklehurst made most effective flank movement driving Boers back a considerable distance. Feel very proud that one of my Equerries should have done so well. The position at Ladysmith is considered quite safe & there are plenty of good stores of all kinds".

In fact, as Julian Symons says in his book on *"Bullers Campaigns"*, once the troops had become used to the idea that they were besieged and would be shelled every day their life settled down to a routine in which the chief enemy was not Boers but boredom. The constant shelling from the heights around the town had an effect on morale but the Boers 'Long Toms' were fired from such a distance that the British guns could not reach them and they were comparatively harmless.

The other main problem was the death toll from disease and three field hospitals were set up to care for the victims of typhoid and dysentery. Among them was George Steevens, the special correspondent of *The Daily Mail,* who had written so eloquently of Gordon's memorial and garden and who, until his death from enteric fever, enlivened life in Ladysmith by producing a paper known as the *Ladysmith Lyre.*

Until they began to eat rather than feed the horses the cavalry were the most useful patrol force and White used them to harass the enemy in an attempt to stop them moving south in force. "He has repeatedly out generalled the redoubtable Joubert ....especially after the cleverly planned and executed attack on the Boer camp near Besters in which the cavalry under General Brocklehurst shone so conspicuously." reported the *Daily News,* adding, " Nothing could exceed the dreary monotony of our existence here."

In the meantime Buller had landed at Cape Town with the main force which he considered would be strong enough to overcome the stiffest resistance from the Boers. Once again this was a miscalculation. In what became known as 'Black Week', in December 1899, the British were defeated at Stormberg and Magersfontein and Buller, who was advancing to relieve Ladysmith, was defeated by Louis Botha at Colenso. Buller then panicked, signalling to White that Ladysmith should surrender and cabling the same to the Cabinet in London.

Their response was to sack Buller and recall Lord Roberts to replace him as Commander-in-Chief, with Kitchener as his chief of staff. Roberts then ordered Buller to do nothing until they arrived in January, despite which Buller attempted one last victory at Spion Kop, only to suffer one of the worst defeats inflicted on British troops since the Crimea, before his advance to relieve Ladysmith.

By February the food supplies in the besieged town were dwindling. 'We might have held out under famine for a week, but hardly longer' wrote the war correspondent of the *Daily News*. "Horseflesh has already been used instead of beef and another concoction for meat extracts. Horse soup - 'chevril' - is in great demand, but without bread, biscuits, peaches and meal these foods would have been barely sufficient to stave off starvation for another week.

"The first sight of the British troops marching to our relief on the 28th February was when it was nearly dark, but the people thronged about the drift where the coming column must cross the river. Lord Dundonald who was at their head was welcomed by General Brocklehurst. When his name was heard the cheering was louder than ever, for he was already well known here in connection with his daring leadership of the irregular horse."

On the 1st March the garrison reverted to a full half-ration of biscuits and horseflesh and on the 3rd March the relieving army headed by Buller made its triumphal entry into Ladysmith and, passing the town, encamped on the plain beyond. Brocklehurst cabled Queen Victoria - "Gen: Buller has just ridden in, his face was fair to look upon" which she noted "made us laugh very much." He also cabled and wrote to Louie: "Buller just in and we are precious glad to see him as you may imagine. I shall not attempt to describe the last 4 months as they have been disagreeable very, not to say dull and so it would be unprofitable - yarns improve with keeping so they can wait. "I only heard a moment ago that a mail was going so this must be short as time is nearly up, but I have sent you and Her Majesty (the two most important people to me) a cable apiece. HM and I have exchanged 4 cables, her first enquiring after my health!

It does seem so odd writing a letter again which is to go beyond the outpost and also to think that we shall be reading letters in a few days. I am looking forward so to yours my sweet darling and hope you put in lots about the farm, mares, yearlings etc. (I quite sympathise with the Boers wanting to get back to their farms). Fallow galloped in this morning full of life and talk and left me a flask of whisky with which I will drink your very good health tonight. Dear old Buller asked me to dine with him at their camp 4 miles off and said he would give me a bottle of pop, but I can't get away as fighting is still going on and some of my men are out.

Four-fifths of my horses have been eaten and very good they were - the soup thereof is called 'chevril' and otherwise they were the only meat you could get your teeth through. I've been well all the time, but most of my staff have been ill at one time or another."

There was obviously a lull in the fighting after Ladysmith was relieved, with a chance for the cavalry to acquire more horses, and the next news we have of Brocklehurst is a cable to Queen Victoria at the beginning of May saying: "At last things are moving, but have nothing definite to report. The rest has quite set my men up again but Brigade has had to be entirely remounted."

By the beginning of June he was reporting to the Queen that his Brigade was with General
Lyttleton and on 12th June he cabled her from Volksrust "My Brigade arrived here today with General Buller via Botha's pass".

Still with Buller he wrote to Louie from Charleston "It is rather a weary world here today - the grass all burnt having been fired by the Boers, so the country round is black with a background of mountain and stones. It is raining and blowing hard, which means the men will get wet through, it will freeze hard tonight on top of it, and we have no tents, yet no one says anything and there is no grumbling. I think I've got all your letters dear old thing and the one today was a blessing as things are beastly all round. A few sinister reports about Bobs [Lord Roberts] are flying about, but nothing authentic and as Bobs is not loved by the Bosses here one has to take the stories with much salt."

Louie had apparently been upset by some reports from the Ladies Relief Committee at Cape Town, which had been organised by Lady Edward Cecil to care for the women and children who were refugees from the Rand. Brocklehurst reassured her that their ideas were foolish: "From all accounts the Ladies at Cape Town are a lot of silly women who probably don't mean any harm but want slapping and sending home to make them see their folly."

"Goodnight old darling", he ended. "I wish I had your bed to creep into tonight - with you in it."

The following day he wrote again, saying things were improving: "The wind has dropped and the sun has come up, so everything is drying and perking up again. My Brigade are being very hard worked - patrols and escorts - reconnaissance - and the horses only get bad oats or grass and are going back fast this cold weather. I am getting anxious about them - I hope to get them a hay ration of sorts today or tomorrow. News just in that things are going right with Bobs again and that we are to march on Wednesday to dislodge a force of Boers north of us, when this is done if Bobs has really cleared Pretoria it is difficult to see what more there is to do - and the home trek ought soon to begin.

June 19th - another pause, as there is no enemy in front of us - so Buller goes to Standerton with 3 Brigades and leaves Gen. Hildy at Volksrust, Gen. Lyttleton at Laings Nek and Ingogo, and me at Charleston. Buller says he will not move until he has 40 days supplies at Volksrust, but that then he will go on with the lot of us to Pretoria. This means my being here for pretty nearly another week."

By August Brocklehurst and his brigade had reached Helvetia near Machadadorp and reported "My General, Buller has done a big thing the last 3 weeks, ending up by releasing the prisoners at Noigedocht yesterday. There was fighting all the way from Parade Kop (near Volksrust) but Monday's fight (a tough one) knocked the Boers out and drove them into the wild country. "There were many gruesome sights on Monday, but there are some nice dog episodes. A spaniel led the final assault and was first into position. I saw a dog and his master lying side by side, both killed (as I daresay you know every soldier keeps a dog if he can get hold of one); also several wounded men being taken care of by their dogs until the doctors came round. One dog, a terrier, sat with his dead master all night close to where I slept and would not come away. So we fed him where he was, poor beast, and when they fetched the man I took the dog and have him now."

A telegram from Lord Roberts on the 8th September announced that Dundonald and Brocklehurst occupied Lyndenberg yesterday afternoon. Buller and Hamilton's forces were within five miles of the town. Brocklehurst wrote to Louie from Lyndenberg. "Just a line in a big hurry to say we arrived here yesterday - or rather my advance guard arrived on the 6th - a Long Tom opened on my main body on the far hills to the east so I bivouacked there out of range until the army came up - it is a nice little town in a wild country full of clear streams and I got the Union Jack on the flagstaff about 9 am yesterday and very well it looked.

Darling old thing I have tried hard to get cables thro' to you but there has been such a rush and crush I haven't succeeded. I left Buller on Monday last to join Ian Hamilton on his turning movement and had to get through a very bad country to join him - in fact we had a v.rough time for 5 days. I join on to Buller again today but I do not yet know what the next move will be. The infantry are just going to attack some Boers to the east of the town who have 2 Long Toms and my brigade is just moving out to support them on the South so I must close.

I have an idea that it would be rather nice when I come back to come to the same rooms in Hans Crescent Hotel from which I started and you just to wait there for me to turn up and open the door to come in as I opened it to go out - what do you think you sweet thing? - arrange it if it fits as we should be very comfy whenever I was inside and there would be no idiots about.

Best love my darling and hoping I may be opening that door before long."

CHAPTER FOURTEEN

The war had released a great wave of patriotism in England. As the army under Lord Roberts' command reversed their earlier defeats, news of the relief of Ladysmith and Mafeking was greeted with national rejoicing on every street corner and households up and down the country seemed to join the march 'With the Flag to Pretoria'. Macclesfield was delighted to have a war hero in Brocklehurst and the Mayor telegraphed the town's congratulations to him on the relief of Ladysmith, receiving in reply the rather laconic 'Many thanks'.

As Louie anxiously waited for his return to England the *'Macclesfield Courier'* reported that Major - General Brocklehurst would return from South Africa as soon as his services could be spared, to resume his duty as Equerry to the Queen.

'Macclesfield's brilliant son has well earned a rest from the turmoils of war, for ever since going out to South Africa, he has, to use an expressive phrase, been "in the thick of it". His splendid services in the defence of Ladysmith, through the terrible siege, have even been excelled, if that were possible, by the masterly manner in which, under General Ian Hamilton, he has co-operated with General Buller in the movements which have resulted in the bloodless capture of Lyndenberg and I am sure that I am only echoing the sentiments of every citizen in loyal Macclesfield when I say that a visit by General

Brocklehurst to the town of his birth would be greeted with unbounded enthusiasm. We want to congratulate and honour him'.

Two years later, on the 6th October 1902, they made him an Honorary Freeman of Macclesfield and presented him with a magnificent solid silver casket engraved with his arms and a list of his battles. Its cover surmounted by the figure of victory, the casket was supported by four lions resting on an oak base. Truly a gift for a hero.

In the meantime, however, although Bloemfontein, Johannesburg and Pretoria had been captured, the war had not yet been won. Lord Roberts and General Buller returned to England, leaving Kitchener in command in South Africa where the Boers continued to fight a determined guerrilla campaign.

Brocklehurst had arrived back in time to take his turn as equerry at Windsor before the Court removed to Osborne. On the 27 November 1900 Queen Victoria recorded in her Journal that General Brocklehurst dined with her at Windsor: He "...has just returned from S.Africa & looks quite unchanged, never having had a day's ill health. He also praised dear Christle [Prince Christian Victor of Schleswig-Holstein, the Queen's soldier grandson] whom he had seen a great deal of, very much". The Prince had died of typhoid in Pretoria the month before.

Brocklehurst, who had been awarded the CB for his services in South Africa, soon found himself involved with Rhodes and Stead in trying to bring the war to an end. Stead had always been violently opposed to the war, using his journal 'War Against War' to mobilise public opinion against the fighting.

His interest in South Africa had developed through his friendship with Cecil Rhodes during the 1890s, when Rhodes came to London in 1889 seeking support for his British South Africa Company. From their first luncheon meeting the two men were filled with enthusiasm for each other and Stead became the strongest propagandist for Rhodes and his ambitions. In return Rhodes bought into Stead's newspaper the *Pall Mall Gazette*, which was in some financial difficulty at the time, and thereafter provided him with steady support.

When Stead left the *Pall Mall Gazette* in 1890 and founded his *Review of Reviews* he continued to promote Rhodes to the British public and the latter's visits to England and his naming of Stead as a trustee of his wills of 1891, 1892 and 1893 compounded their friendship, until this was threatened by the disastrous Jameson Raid and Stead's attempts to extricate Rhodes from any blame in the affair.

Presumably Brocklehurst met Rhodes through Stead and when Stead was trying to justify the raid on the grounds that his arch enemy Joseph Chamberlain, the Colonial Secretary, had connived in planning the conspiracy, Brocklehurst was concerned to learn that the officers who had taken part in the raid were in danger of being deprived of their commissions.

The historian Joseph O Baylen who has researched and written extensively on the subject, particularly in his 'W T Stead's *History of the Mystery* and the Jameson Raid' says that Hawksley (Rhodes'solicitor) gave Brocklehurst copies of the cables which had passed from the Colonial Office to the officers. When Brocklehurst in turn showed these to General Sir Redvers Buller at the War Office, Buller was so impressed that he told Brocklehurst to ask Sir John Willoughby to draft a letter stating that he and his officers had followed Jameson upon being informed that they were acting 'on the Queen's service'. Willoughby wrote the letter but the matter was subsequently quashed by the Colonial Office and the officers' commissions were revoked.

Central to this part of the drama was Edmund Garrett, who was one of Stead's 'disciples' on the *Pall Mall Gazette*. When Garrett developed tuberculosis Stead sent him to South Africa as the newspaper's correspondent there and later, with the support of both Rhodes and Stead, he became editor in 1895 of Rhodes' newspaper the *Cape Times*. At first Garrett joined Stead in supporting Rhodes after the Jameson Raid, but when Stead continued to press against Chamberlain and the Colonial Office, Garrett appeared to change sides and to refute Stead's charges and insinuations. Brocklehurst was particularly angry at his criticism of the army officers who took part in the raid and wrote to Stead: "I do not want his opinion on W [Willoughby], or on patriotism, or on sedition, neither do I want an abject apology. What I do want is that, knowing as I do, that his imputing blackmail intentions to W's letter to the War Office is unjust, that he should withdraw that imputation."

The subsequent political intrigues and the publication of Stead's *History of a Mystery* led to a parliamentary enquiry and to Rhodes finally agreeing not to produce the cables incriminating Joseph Chamberlain and the Colonial Office, in return for a pledge from Chamberlain to protect his Chartered Company. They also transformed Stead from being anti-Boer to pro-Boer. 'Denounced by the jingoes as a liar and a traitor and deserted by many who had long admired his honest dissent, Stead became one of the most hated men in England.' How he reconciled his campaign against the war with his friendship with the fighting cavalry officer is not known, but firm friends he and Brocklehurst remained.

When Brocklehurst came back from his war service he heard that, following the British successes in South Africa, and believing the war to be all but over, Rhodes had agreed to address a meeting at Cape Town of the South African League, a group of loyal propagandists, and he used the occasion to emphasise his belief in the union of the people of South Africa.

"You think you have beaten the Dutch", Rhodes said "But it is not so. The Dutch are not beaten; what is beaten is Krugerism, a corrupt and evil government.....The Dutch are as vigorous and unconquered today as they have ever been; the country is still as much theirs as it is yours, and you will have to live and work with them hereafter as in the past."

The speech was very well received, particularly among his friends in England and Brocklehurst wrote to Rhodes:

"I have been rubbing it into everyone since I got back that you are the only man who can save South Africa (beginning with the Queen) and I am surprised to find how many of your enemies agree. I told the Queen you and Gordon were the same man - only with different methods - this fairly made her jump, but 'she saw my point' as you say. The Government, I am sure, would be only too thankful for you to come out of your tent and give them a lead. I have said you and Milner (the Governor of Cape Colony) are on most cordial terms, so that he would approve.

My line has been - you propose a Federal Parliament right away (no Crown Colonies), yourself at the head of it; compensation for both sides for all damage done during the war, and general amnesty. I've got rather hung up trying to work this out in detail, but that is where Cecil Rhodes comes in, and it would mean peace, or at least an alternative to the present policy of trying to sit on bayonets, which would probably be accepted by the Boer leaders and would bring peace."

Stead was also working on a similar plan, proposing that Rhodes should meet with the Boer leaders and bring the war to an end. Brocklehurst discussed this with Dr Jameson and Hawksley "We decided in solemn conclave on Friday night that Rosebery was the man to give Lord Salisbury a lead on your scheme", Brocklehurst told Stead. "I went down to Mentmore yesterday, where he [Rosebery] was supposed to be, but was not. It seems to me good to play up to this - and we can't get at it too soon. Send for Hawksley to talk it over."

Later he wrote from Osborne, where he was in attendance on the Queen, saying that Earl Grey had the impression that Stead was 'gunning for Rhodes.' Brocklehurst explained that Stead was arbitration mad, but had lucid intervals during one of which he had started the most practical cure for the present state of things. 'I am pushing your proposal for all I am worth here, so don't go and upset your own child in visionary flights with St Paul Kruger.

PS Things are really moving a bit in the right direction, I do believe, on the lines that someone draws Lord Salisbury - Lord Salisbury issues a *Ukase* (nice word) - Rhodes comes out of his tent - Chorus of Peace - The Millenium'.

In the meantime, as the war dragged on, Brocklehurst assured Stead that any suggestion of a settlement giving independence to the Boers was 'absolutely impossible' and could only be achieved with Joe's [Joseph Chamberlain] head on a charger.

All this was soon overshadowed by the death of Queen Victoria on the 22nd January 1901, bringing to an end the longest reign in British history, during which the country had become a powerful and prosperous imperial nation. For some reason the Boers had the impression that Queen Victoria was responsible for the government's hard line on South Africa and Brocklehurst assured Stead that he had impressed on Sir Dighton Probyn, then head of the new King's household, that "the Dutch who want peace are looking for his accession to bring it about."

In March, after two representatives from the Boers in the Cape Colony came to London for talks with Joseph Chamberlain and the government, Brocklehurst reported to Stead that their visit had 'hardened wavering hearts and upset our little cart.' The cart was indeed upset and the war continued until the Boers finally surrendered. By the Peace of Vereeniging in May 1902 the Boer republics were absorbed into the British Empire with a promise of self-government, which was honoured in 1907.

Rhodes died a month before the peace settlement, and in his Will endowed 170 distinguished scholarships which bear his name at Oxford, for students from the Colonies, the USA and Germany. Brocklehurst who had just returned from a visit to the Danish court told Stead he had read the latter's paper about Rhodes' Will in the *Review of Reviews* "also used it freely on my attack on the anti-Rhodes direction out there - a strong one. Thanks to my violence, your paper and his Will, I left them all on their backs."

During the last 18 months of the war Kitchener had succeeded in breaking the Boers' resistance only by the ruthless use of blockhouses and concentration camps for civilians. He burnt and looted the farms and the women and children were interned in camps along the railway lines. More than 20,000 Boer civilians died of epidemics in the 'concentration camps'.

Like many of the army officers who had served in South Africa Brocklehurst had a sneaking liking and sympathy for the

Boers, but he lost patience with some of Stead's stories of British misdeeds versus Boer magnanimity. "The fact is" he moralised, as he had done in the desert in the past, "war is war and a very nasty, beastly, dirty undignified business at the best." When Stead quoted accusations of barbarity made against Kitchener by a British officer whose identity he concealed, Brocklehurst condemned him for 'stabbing in the dark'. "It is not your way of doing business" he wrote. "Tell your 'unblemished one' to come into the open if he wants honest men to follow him."

He reacted fiercely in support of officers of the Guards regiments over a case of 'ragging' which had been widely reported in the press. "Granted the ragging was overdone it must be remembered that if you are to have a good Regiment it is absolutely indispensable within bounds", he told Stead. "The Old Blues were always celebrated for their rigorous and successful treatment of 'cubs', but yet I can honestly say that nothing but good ever resulted. I may remark that the Senior Officers of our Army are nearly always men who have risen by Staff work and have little knowledge or sympathy with regimental life - they know a good Regiment when they see one, but have little idea what a delicate organism it is. This idea that is being put about that an officer becomes unpopular by being a keen soldier is absolutely untrue, at least my experience is absolutely the reverse".

He added as a postscript the fact that the Foot Guards were at a disadvantage in having no barracks life in London but that he had been told "over and over again by Linesmen in South Africa that they considered the cheerful and downright and thorough way in which the Guards officers did their duty was a pattern to the Army."

Apparently the 1st Battalion of the Guards had acted as Depot for the 2nd and 3rd Battalions - all young officers passing through the 1st Battalion, with the result that the proportion of older subalterns to 'cubs' was completely upset and at the time of the incidents reported there had only been two or three subalterns of any standing and the young 'cubs' who remained at home were completely out of hand. "Our Army and our War Office, I think you will admit is about as rotten as it can be, but we have one good thing left and that is our Regimental system" Brocklehurst insisted. "Is this to be levelled down to the rest? You may take it from me that if they will only treat a few more officers as they have treated Kinlock they will very soon arrive at this result - I know of what I speak as I was a Regimental Officer for 26 years and know as much about 'ragging' as most people."

He had earlier addressed Stead's other main concern which was with the physical and mental health of Queen Victoria in the months before her death, following some bizarre articles in the American press.

"I can only say I talked to HM for half an hour or more in December after dinner and do not believe she was ever more intellectually able in her life." Brocklehurst wrote. "I sat next but one to her at dinner also, that night and she joined freely in the conversation and laughed heartily at my eulogies of horseflesh. I did not see her to speak to in January, as she was not allowed down, but I know she was looking forward to her trip to France, and there was some animated discussion between her and Sir James Reid as to whether she was equal to the journey or not - He taking the view that as she was doing so well it was inadvisable to risk so long and tiring a journey. Latterly she slept a great deal and was encouraged in every way

to do so.   I believe physically she was sound in all her organs."
In a further letter he said "A propos the Queen's death I should
say the dominant note was that she meant to die QUEEN
without a shadow of Regency."

CHAPTER FIFTEEN

Since the early Norman kings no man has been so frequently crowned as Colonel John Fielden Brocklehurst of the Royal Horse Guards", reported the journal *Modern Society*. Following the death of Queen Victoria Brocklehurst had transferred effortlessly to become Equerry to Queen Alexandra and "during the final preparations and rehearsals at the Abbey [for the Coronation], he so handsomely, in every sense of the word, represented His Majesty and acted as understudy to King Edward VII. He, if anyone, should be able to tell 'how uneasy lies the Head that wears the Crown' and his vacuous experience might have sent a weaker and more excitable person searching for a throne for the rest of his life". It was the first time on record that the Majesty of England had been represented.

Brocklehurst himself had quipped during the rehearsals, after receiving the homage of the Archbishop of Canterbury, Frederick Temple, that the last time he had come into close personal contact with the great churchman had been on receiving a flogging at his hands at Rugby some 35 years before.

In the event, on the eve of the Coronation the ceremony had to be postponed for the King to be operated on for acute appendicitis. He had been extremely unwilling to postpone his crowning and against the advice of the eminent surgeons Sir Frederick Treves, Lord Lister and Sir Thomas Barlow he initially refused the operation, saying he could not disappoint the nation - he was determined to go to Westminster Abbey. "Then, Sire you will go there as a dead man" Treves is said to have told him. Reluctantly the King consented. Treves telegraphed the London Hospital, where he was a Senior Surgeon, to send a nurse to Buckingham Palace at once and an improvised room was prepared for the emergency operation from which the King made an uneventful recovery. The Coronation finally took place two months later.

Before becoming Queen Alexandra's Equerry there is nothing to suggest that Brocklehurst and Louie were ever part of the 'Marlborough set' although the Hon Oliver Montagu who had preceded Brocklehurst as Commander of the Blues was reputed to have loved Queen Alexandra 'with exalted, chivalrous and selfish passion' and his death in 1893 'left in her heart an aching void which was never filled'.

In 1867, five days before the birth of her daughter Princess Louise, her third child, the Queen, then Princess of Wales, became seriously ill with rheumatic fever which left her with a slight but permanent limp and otosclerosis, a form of progressive deafness. This hearing loss gradually made the social life which she had enjoyed more and more difficult, although she was clever at disguising and circumventing the problem. By the time her husband succeeded to the throne the centre of her life had shifted from the social whirl of London to Sandringham; to her children and grandchildren, her dogs and horses and the delights of country living.

Her biographer Georgina Battiscombe describes her life at Sandringham 'Visiting "my poor people", keeping a benevolent eye on the school she had established for boys on the estate, arguing with gardeners who preferred grand bedding out displays to "my poor innocent inexpensive little flowers" and discussing church and parish affairs with the local parson.'

Brocklehurst fitted well into such a world and he was to become her sole Equerry. Writing to offer him the appointment on the 21st February 1901 Sir Dighton Probyn, Keeper of the Privy Purse said 'The pay I am sorry to say is small - only £300 a year - but then on the other hand the office will, I should think be almost a sinecure whereas the King's equerries will have a hard time of it occasionally.'

Still deeply in love with his wife Brocklehurst never displayed the slavish devotion to Queen Alexandra of Oliver Montagu, although he did become her loyal and trusted friend. In a letter to him on 12th March 1904 she thanks him for 'y^{re}. most charmingly worded wishes for our Wedding day - the 41st!!! I too am very grateful to the Fates for having given me such an excellent Equerry as you are!!!'

In the meantime WT Stead was not the only member of his family to try and take advantage of Brocklehurst's Royal connections. His third son, Alfred had spent his honeymoon in Japan and was ardently pro-Japanese. When Marquis Ito Hirobumi, the Japanese Prime Minister and Special Envoy to Europe visited London in the winter of 1901-02 Alfred Stead tried to enlist Brocklehurst's help in obtaining decorations for Ito and his minister Mr Tsudzuki, and in arranging for them to be received at Sandringham by the King and Queen.

Brocklehurst willingly obliged and Ito was awarded the GCB, but the command to visit Sandringham failed through the meddling of the Foreign Office and the Japanese Legation.

Explaining the circumstances to Brocklehurst in a letter,

Alfred Stead said that the Royal Command to Sandringham had come to Baron Hayashi, the Japanese Ambassador, in the form of a query as to whether Marquis Ito could postpone his departure from England for a few days so that he could visit the King and Queen at Sandringham. As soon as Baron Hayashi received this he went straight to Lord Lansdowne and Mr Barrington of the Foreign Office and asked what he should do. The Foreign Office and the Ambassador then put their heads together to prevent Ito going to Sandringham. "As I have already pointed out to the Baron's superiors this was a gross breach of etiquette and quite inexcusable", Alfred Stead wrote. "If their Majesties were good enough to approach the Japanese visitors directly it was not for these latter to bring in the Foreign Office. Hayashi will be severely censored from Tokyo, but alas harm is already done. Both Marquis Ito and Mr. Tsudsuki are most disappointed not to have gone."

Brocklehurst had also apparently succeeded in annoying Lord Lansdowne through by-passing him in the award of GCB to Marquis Ito. "I think that you managed the decoration magnificently - GCB was splendid and the Marquis is overjoyed", Alfred Stead told Brocklehurst. "I pointed out to him how much he missed by not being invested by His Majesty and how badly he had treated all who had secured his command. Really it seems as if one must remain all the time beside him if one would be sure that no *betises* will be made. I am sure that the GCB will be of the greatest service to England in the Far East, all the more so as it was so unexpected. I succeeded in making Marquis Ito very sorry for himself and most angry with Baron Hayashi for his stupidity," he wrote. "Please be assured of my deep regret at what has happened. If there is anything the Marquis should do I will see that he does it."

This was not quite the end of Brocklehurst's affair with the Japanese as the following year, 1903, presumably once again at the request of Alfred Stead, he was discussing with Fritz Ponsonby and Francis Knollys, the King's Private Secretaries, the suggestion that the Emperor of Japan should be made a Knight of the Garter. Ponsonby wrote to Brocklehurst that this would be impossible in view of the strained relations between Japan and Russia. [Queen Alexandra's sister was Dowager Empress of Russia and Queen Victoria's Granddaughter Alix the present Empress and by 1904 Japan and Russia were at war]. 'I told him (Francis Knollys) of your suggestion of a birthday or some other non-political date being chosen, but he said that as the Emperor of Japan had not been on a visit to England, and as the Garter had never been given before, it would certainly be misinterpreted by Russia if the present time was chosen to send a deputation to present the Garter to the Japanese Emperor.   'The real difficulty however has been the Sultan of Turkey who has become dissatisfied ever since the Shah was given the Garter. It is apparently not considered advisable to let him [the Japanese Emperor] have the Garter until he comes here or the King goes there. If a Garter is sent to Japan it might make it impossible to refuse the Sultan who has literally asked for it.'

After this you would have thought that Brocklehurst would have had his fill of diplomatic overtures, but that would never be likely while he and WT Stead were friends, and in August 1905 they left together for Russia, where Stead was on a mission to support the establishment of a constitutional monarchy and avert the threat of revolution.

Popular discontent in Russia fuelled by heavy taxation and the country's defeat in the Russo-Japanese War had led to a peaceful demonstration in St.Petersburg which was fired on by troops. The crew of the battleship *Potemkin* mutinied and a workers' council was formed prompting the Tsar Nicholas II to promise the formation of an elected assembly - the Douma.

Stead realised that his mission to Russia would be useless unless he was received by the Tsar and his relationship with Brocklehurst proved an ideal opportunity to make this possible. "As the disorders in Russia mounted during July 1905 and menaced the security of the Imperial Family .....Queen Alexandra became increasingly concerned for the safety of her sister Marie Fedorovna., the Dowager Empress of Russia", and it was easy for Brocklehurst to persuade the Queen to allow him to go to Russia and escort the Empress to their family home in Copenhagen. Princess Victoria, who was godmother to the Tsarevich (the Tsar's son and heir) was also anxious that Brocklehurst should go and ensure that the family was safe.

It is difficult to decide at this point who was using whom to further their purposes. Stead maintained that to avoid the appearance that the British Royal Family was supporting the Tsar in any conflict with his subjects, he had arranged to go to Russia and provide a screen for Brocklehurst's visit. In return Brocklehurst would accompany Stead to St Petersburg and ensure that he had audiences with the Dowager Empress and the Tsar and Stead would help to pay his own expenses by writing articles on Russia for an American press syndicate and *The Times* and *Daily News* of London.

On arriving in Russia Stead found that one of the stumbling blocks to his plan was that the Russian liberals would not listen to him until he could secure the release of one of their leaders, Professor Miliukov, Professor of History and leader of the Constitutional Democrat Party, who had been arrested in his house as he was discussing the proposed Douma with some of his delegates and 'clapped into gaol' on suspicion of contemplating political crime. 'What use was the Douma under a despot?' his party wanted to know.

On the 28th August Stead and Brocklehurst went by train to Peterhof on the Gulf of Finland where the Romanov family had their summer palace - Stead for his audience with the Dowager Empress and Brocklehurst to lunch with the Tsar and see the baby Tsarevich.

Stead's intention in his audience with the Dowager Empress was to persuade her to use her considerable influence with the Tsar to stick to his proposal to form a Douma.

He was somewhat dismayed however when she did not send the promised carriage to meet him at the station. Fortunately he was able to travel with Brocklehurst, who dropped him off at the small palace where the Dowager Empress was staying, before continuing to his lunch with the Tsar.

Stead recalled driving behind two black horses down a longish driveway through the Park - "Here and there a sentry paced up and down, but there was no more outward and visible sign of precautions than at Windsor Castle. Children played about. You passed one or two monster Circassians, a labouring man or two carrying dinner in a handkerchief, a youth on a bicycle, ragged hedges, some wooden pilings.....At last the palace, a pretty country villa embodied in flowers and foliage."

Although Stead had had dealings with Nicholas II before, most notably during the Hague Convention, this was to be his first meeting with the Tsar's mother. She was shorter than he expected, without the graceful elegance of her sister, Queen Alexandra, and by no means as beautiful, but "she had expressive eyes which when lit up by a smile often entirely transfigured her face....and she had an air of will and intelligence".

As the audience progressed Stead told her he had heard a great deal about her from Colonel Brocklehurst. "Oh is he not charming", she exclaimed, "so delightful. He is my very ideal of a true Englishman". and later, "he is so good and true", she remarked. Stead told her "....I am here really because he wanted so much to come and see you. He told me long ago you had asked him to come. But it was difficult, so I invented a visit for myself to come in order that he might travel as my friend and it would not cause any complication."

Having succeeded in arranging this audience with the Dowager he wanted to use it to ensure that the proposed formation of the Douma "should be carried through logically and no turning back". They enjoyed a free and frank discussion, but Stead failed to gain an undertaking from her that she would 'stiffen' the Tsar in his position on the Douma and he then became concerned that by meeting her he might have compromised his position with the Tsar. However, on discussing the outcome with Brocklehurst he decided that he had done right to trust her. "Brocklehurst also believes I have done right", he wrote after the audience, "and have not said one word which I ought not to have said. He thinks she is unscrupulous. But her interest lies in keeping faith with me. She has nothing to gain by betraying me."

It was just over a fortnight later that Stead had his audience with Nicholas II, and by this time Brocklehurst had returned to England to escort Queen Alexandra to her family home in Denmark, where the Dowager Empress later joined them. Stead waited anxiously in St Petersburg for his audience with the Tsar which had been promised and put off. "The visit of the Shah and the conclusion of the peace had postponed everything and some friends were lugubriously declaring the appointment was off."

He told Brocklehurst to describe to the Dowager Empress how he had been feeling like Vania - a character from Grinka's opera 'Life for the Tsar'- left 'waiting at the gate' until on his return from the opera he found a message that the Tsar would receive him the following day.

Stead wrote a detailed account of his audience with the Tsar, which was summed up by Brocklehurst in a letter to King Edward VII.   "I hope Your Majesty received my cable saying that my Friend had had a two hours interview [with the Tsar]. I heard last night that the conference scheme and propaganda are not only to be permitted but will be encouraged - The Emperor is revising the Speech [which Stead proposed to give at a public conference on the Douma] himself, during his Cruise and The Empress [Queen Victoria's granddaughter] will revise articles to be written to "The Times". The Emperor would not say good bye, as he said he would see him again and he wished him (Stead) to see The Ministers and every body. The three liberties speech Press and association will be conceded, with a limited Habeas Corpus. - there will also be a Cabinet and a Prime Minister. The Emperor means to go about more and will see members of the Douma.

The Professor Melukoff (Chicago University) of whom I spoke, was in Gaol without The Emperor's knowledge and is now liberated. - The Emperor also discussed General Booth [founder of the Salvation Army] - the Welsh Revival - Baku and Mr Stead's Gaol experiences. [According to General Booth Russia and the North Pole were at that time the only two places in the world where the Salvation Army could not go]. I enclose an article by Mr Stead to The Russian Press - the only one I have translated. It was his third, but will give Your Majesty an idea of the line he is taking."

Stead's own verbatim records of his audiences with the Dowager Empress and the Tsar were not published until 1969 when the historian and Stead's biographer, Joseph O Baylen published them in his research paper '*The Tsar's "Lecturer-General."* W T Stead and the Russian Revolution of 1905' for the School of Arts and Sciences at Georgia State College Atlanta Georgia.

From this we learn that during the audience with the Tsar he underlined to Stead the affection in which Brocklehurst was held by the Romanov family.

What a nice man, Colonel Brocklehurst is", he told him. "I met him quite a long time ago. He was then Colonel of the Blues, I think. It was before I had married and I was staying at Kingston [where the Brocklehurst's had a house] for a month and naturally it was a very happy time". On his recent visit to the Tsar's family Brocklehurst had "not only seen the Tsarevich, but had him in his arms" (the tone implied that this was something very great).

However, Brocklehurst was wrong to give the King the impression that Professor Miliukov had been released for on 24th September Stead wrote that he was "still in doubt whether Miliukoff is to be let out and until he is let out I wont go on the stump". He enclosed a copy of the speech he was proposing to deliver in Russia "wherever there are people who might hear me" in support of the Tsar and the Douma.

It was not until 28th September that a triumphant letter came to Brocklehurst declaring that Professor Miliukov had been freed at last and crediting the spirits of Alexander and General

Gordon for supporting his campaign 'from the other side'. "I think we shall save our Khartoum now", he commented.

Unfortunately this was not so. By this time Stead had been asked by the Tsar not to hold public conferences as he had planned and although he went about Russia preaching patriotic co-operation and acting as propagandist and 'spin doctor' for the Tsar the task of reconciling the Russian progressives and the reactionaries was beyond his power. Even Miliukov dissasociated himself from Stead and denied that Stead's intervention had achieved his release from gaol.

Stead returned to London in November, a disappointed saviour of the Russian cause, where his intervention had been a failure. When after Stead's death and many years later Brocklehurst asked Dr. A J Dillon whether Stead's mission to Russia had been too late he replied, " No, not too late. If only the suggestions then made had been hearkened to, all that has happened since [the Russian Revolution and the slaughter of the Romanov family] would have been avoided".

CHAPTER SIXTEEN

Yours till hell freezes" read the letter. The signatory was 'Jack' Fisher - Admiral Sir John Fisher - who became 1st Sea Lord in 1904 and was a close friend of Brocklehurst. This sign off was typical of his joking and flamboyant style, although Fritz Ponsonby claimed that Fisher had adopted the phrase from him after he, in turn, had first seen it used in a letter from an officer in India.

Fisher was an energetic and impetuous man. At the time of his appointment as 1st Sea Lord the Navy was split into two factions - between Fisher and the Commander-in-Chief of the Channel Fleet, Lord Charles Beresford. 'Both wanted a Navy ready to meet the German challenge', but similar to the previous schism in the Army between the Duke of Cambridge and Lord Wolseley -Beresford believed in tradition and orthodoxy while Fisher wanted reform, particularly advocating promotion on merit rather than seniority. He also championed the *Dreadnought* - a new type of heavily armed battleship and demanded that as many as four should be built in the race to ensure that the British Navy was better equipped than the Germans.

In his battle for the expansion and modernisation of the Navy he was always backed by King Edward VII, who had earlier fallen out with Beresford after they had publicly quarrelled over their respective liaisons with Daisy Brooke - Countess of Warwick.

Queen Alexandra, although she seldom interfered in politics, was also one of Fisher's 'most ardent partisans'. "Fisher wrote, spoke and thought in large type italics" according to his friend Admiral Sir Roger Bacon and Queen Alexandra's letters reveal that she had much in common with him - both were enthusiastic, impetuous and single-minded and laughed at the same jokes.

Brocklehurst's friendship with Fisher developed when they were both included in the Royal party which sailed on the Royal yacht *Victoria & Albert* in 1908 to Revel in Russia to meet the entire Russian Imperial Family in their yachts *Standard* and *Polar Star*.

"The King has sweetly asked me to go to Russia with him which is lovely", Fisher wrote. "And the Queen has telegraphed for the Grand Duchess I am in love with to come and meet me". [The Grand Duchess was the youngest sister of the Tsar, whom Fisher had met the previous year at Carlsbad, where he had taught her to waltz, much to the King's amusement.]

Brocklehurst reported on the Russian visit to Stead, who wrote it up in a character sketch of Fisher published in the *Review of Reviews*. "I have heard from one who was present that he was the life and soul of the party, that he charmed everyone by the gaiety of his conversation, that he even succeeded in achieving the impossible by bringing a smile to the face of the Empress of Russia. But what I should most have liked to see was the dance which was improvised after the State Banquet when the band struck up the waltz in *"The Merry Widow"*. The Grand Duchess Olga and Admiral Fisher danced with their hands behind their heads, with all the brilliant company standing around the dancers until they were tired. Then 'Jackie' went on deck and by requests, which were commands, he brought down the house by dancing a hornpipe".

On their return to England the Grand Duchess wrote to Fisher saying; "What a nice time we had at Revel wasn't it? All our gentlemen - ministers, admirals and generals were delighted with you, as you brought such an amount of frolic and jollity into their midst. They couldn't get over it and spoke about you and your dancing, anecdotes. etc. without end. I told them that even if they tried their very hardest they would never reach anywhere near your level. I shall never forget the last evening when you entertained [Princess] Victoria, Brocklehurst and me with your solo performance. I hadn't laughed so much for ages."

Fisher and Brocklehurst were to remain great friends and in the meantime the latter found his own family were also anxious to exploit his place at Court. It was through him that his cousin Edith Talbot was invited to become a lady-in-waiting to Queen Alexandra. Her granddaughter, Lettice Miller, says Edith refused the honour, as she did not want to be away from her husband during his holidays. "It was such a pity", she said "as she had such a terrific cult for the Queen, but she might not have been very happy, as I believe Alexandra only had the tall, pretty ladies for the Ascot and Cowes waitings - the others had to be content with Balmoral, which was frightfully uncomfortable - I fear this would have been poor Grannie's lot as she was rather short and not particularly good looking."

Another cousin, the twenty-year old Sir Philip Brocklehurst was about to set off with Ernest Shackleton on his 1907-1909 Antarctic Expedition and hoped that a word in the right direction at Court might result in Royal patronage for the expedition, to which he had already committed significant funds from his inheritance. Although Brocklehurst failed to achieve Royal patronage, he was able to arrange for Shackleton and the members of his expedition aboard their ship the *Nimrod* to be commanded to Cowes during Cowes Week, where they were given a Royal send-off by the King and Queen, together with the Prince of Wales (later King George V), the Princess of Wales, the Duke of Connaught, Princess Victoria and Prince Edward (later King Edward VIII). It is also likely that, following the King's presentation of the Royal Victorian Order to Shackleton, the Queen's graceful gift to him of a flag, with a note attached which read, 'May this Union Jack, which I entrust to your keeping lead you safely to the South Pole' had been prompted by her equerry Brocklehurst. Later he organised cables from the King to Shackleton to speed him on his journey as the Nimrod left Christchurch in New Zealand on 1st January 1907 on the start of this new adventure.

Brocklehurst was still spending as much time as he could at Ranksborough and in 1906 he was appointed Lord Lieutenant of Rutland at the suggestion of the then Liberal Prime Minister, Campbell-Bannerman. "He is I believe not a supporter of the Government, but we all know him to be a broad-minded man", he wrote to the King's Private Secretary, Francis Knollys.

Two years later, in 1908, Brocklehurst retired from the Army with the honorary rank of Major-General. He took his equine duties at Court very seriously. He was considered to be one of the finest horsemen in the country, and horses chosen by him were soon being transported to Royal households across Europe. Queen Alexandra's daughter, Maud, who had married her cousin Prince Charles, later King Haakon of Norway, wrote to remind him of his promise to 'look out for a small pony' for her son Olav.....''I fear I am giving you a great deal of trouble and bother, but I hope you will forgive me", she wrote. "Olav is looking forward to it and will be most grateful to the friendly 'Big Soldier Man'. He was asked to send the pony from Hull by sea to Christiana - "they look after horses so well on the Wilson Line."

Sometime later Queen Victoria's granddaughter Victoria Eugenie (Ena), daughter of Princess Beatrice and Prince Henry of Battenberg, who was then Queen of Spain wrote "I can never thank you enough for all the trouble you have taken about my horses. They all arrived safely and in good health two days ago and I am greatly delighted with them. They are just exactly what I wanted and everyone admires them immensely. I go each day to see them and am just longing for the day when I can ride them and hunt on them. I shall have myself photographed on all of them and send them to you. What ages ago it seems to me since I used to go out for rides with you and we went to the meet at Carisbrook!"

It seems likely that Brocklehurst was responsible for introducing many members of the Royal family to fox-hunting - King George V's daughter, Princess Mary, then the Princess Royal, wrote to say how much she looked forward to going out hunting with him and a biographer of Edward VIII (the Duke of Windsor) claimed that he was 'introduced to hunting by an equerry'. Brocklehurst himself was Master of the Cottesmore Hunt for a couple of years.

King Edward VII was not keen on hunting, but he did share Brocklehurst's love of the turf. Brough Scott, the racing journalist, while researching the history of the 1904 Grand

National winner Moiffaa, recently discovered that after the King had bought the giant 17-hand New Zealand horse to race in his colours in the 1905 National, when although hot favourite for the race he fell at Becher's the second time round, he had retired him and gave him to Brocklehurst who later claimed he was the best hack he ever had. Although Moiffaa had an aversion to Newmarket, where Brocklehurst used to enjoy watching the racing from the saddle, the horse behaved well on ceremonial and army occasions. And when Edward VII died in 1910 Brocklehurst rode Moiffaa in his funeral procession at St George's Chapel, Windsor.

In March that year Queen Alexandra wrote to Brocklehurst from the new Royal yacht 'Alexandra' on which she was cruising with her sister off Corfu, wishing him a good holiday in Algiers and hoping that Louie would come back "fully restored to health". "Thank God I have got very good news from Biarritz to day and the King has at last been able to go out again", she wrote..

The King was at Biarritz with his mistress Alice Keppel. The Queen had learned to accept their relationship and feel at ease with Mrs Keppel, but as the King's health deteriorated she rushed back to London and both women were at his bedside when he died on 6 May 1910 after a series of heart attacks.

The funeral was held up for a fortnight because of the Queen's reluctance to part from her husband's body. She was sixteen-years-old when they first met and after 47 years of marriage she was bereft. Whatever his failings as a husband he had been an exhilarating and powerful presence throughout her life.

After the funeral, which was attended by eight kings and an emperor, Queen Alexandra was as unwilling to move out of

Buckingham Palace as she had been to move in there from Marlborough House on Edward's accession. The King had bequeathed Sandringham to her for her lifetime, together with a legacy of £200,000.

Finally, in August 1910 she undertook the move back to Marlborough House. "You cannot think what a painful scene there was when we left it [Buckingham Palace]", Charlotte Knollys, the Queen's Woman of the Bedchamber wrote to "My dear Brock". "All the servants were assembled in the Grand Entrance Hall to say goodbye and they cried and the Queen sobbed. I hope I shall never have to go through such a heart-breaking thing again. And I had to say goodbye to my dear Francis [her brother] and see him go off to Scotland to his new Master. It seems as if we were deserted by everybody now! Princess Victoria returns on Monday and I must say I do pity her - she has been away so much since the King's death that she has yet fully to realize how sad and desolate it all is without him! Goodbye now and God bless you - Give a thought some times to your old and faithful friend -Charlotte Knollys."

Charlotte Knollys had been appointed to Queen Alexandra's household in 1872, when she was Princess of Wales, and over the next 50 years she was to become not just a Woman of the Bedchamber, but also a lifelong friend. During that time she never took a holiday, and after King Edward VII's death the Queen began to rely more and more on her services and those of Dighton Probyn, her Comptroller and Treasurer. Together with the Queen's second daughter Princess Victoria, they made up her small household. The Princess remained unmarried, at first for the lack of suitable suitors, and later because Alexandra very selfishly insisted that she should stay with her mother as a perpetual companion and lady-in-waiting.

Brocklehurst found his equerry duties were curtailed as Queen Alexandra spent most of her time at Sandringham. Charlotte Knollys wrote to wish him "every possible happiness for Xmas and the New Year, but perhaps you do not know how much and how greatly we regret that you seem to have vanished from our midst. I am sure however that it is not your fault and that you will always keep a kindly feeling for Your faithful old friend - Charlotte Knollys".

CHAPTER SEVENTEEN

Royal duties and politics do not usually mix, but with friends like Asquith and W T Stead Brocklehurst often became involved in the political scene, particularly as King George V had inherited not just a throne but also a constitutional crisis. To help deal with this situation the King's Private Secretary, Sir Arthur Bigge had suggested that Francis Knollys, who had been Private Secretary to Edward VII, and who was also friendly with Asquith, should serve with him as Joint Private Secretary with special responsibility for handling the difficult political question.

This had arisen through an attempt by Asquith's Liberal government to curb the veto powers of the obstructive and overwhelming Conservative majority in the House of Lords by introducing a Parliament Bill .Fearful, understandably that the Lords would reject such a Bill, Asquith had asked the King for a secret undertaking that if, as expected, the Liberal party won the impending General Election he would agree to create enough new Liberal peers to swamp the Conservative opposition and ensure the Bill's safe passage through Parliament. On Knollys' advice the King agreed, but in the event the House passed the Parliament Bill with a narrow majority and the King did not need to create a mass of Liberal peers. "Lord Halsbury is quite right - you will spoil the House of Lords if you strengthen it, which is the only change you can make", Brocklehurst commented in a letter to Stead.

He could not have known then that he was soon to become a member of the Upper House himself. In the Birthday Honours List of 1914 he was created a Baron and styled himself Lord Ranksborough of Ranksborough after the gorse-covered hill which stood above the house he had built at Langham in Rutland, becoming the first, and probably the last peer to call himself after a fox's covert.

"My dear General - very many good wishes on your added honour. Long may you live to hunt!" wrote Sir Evelyn Wood. While his Brocklehurst cousins irreverently christened him 'Old Gorsebush'.

The following year Asquith wrote to "My dear Brock - I hope you can see your way to accept the Lordship in Waiting which is about to be vacated by Wimborne. The King is very anxious that you should be his successor - and so am I." Brocklehurst was torn between his affection and loyalty to Queen Alexandra and the prospect of this added royal appointment, but the Queen, although anxious to retain him, felt that she should not stand in his way. He told Asquith "I saw Queen Alexandra yesterday. Her Majesty wishes me to remain in her household, but is willing that I should succeed Wimborne with His Majesty if it is understood that I am ready to return to her service should she at any time wish me to do so. As it is unlikely that Her Majesty will want me in the near future I feel I can safely accept His Majesty's kind offer."

Sometime before this Royal appointment Brocklehurst had lost his long-time friend and correspondent W T Stead. It was probably inevitable that Stead, the consumate newsman, should have decided to travel on the maiden voyage of the great ship *Titanic* and be among the 1,490 who lost their lives when the 'supposedly unsinkable' ship struck an iceberg in the North Atlantic. Telegrams to London, following the disaster, reported that Stead had been at the forefront with the women and children, putting them in the boats. "One can see him, probably singing Hallelujah and encouraging the band to play cheerfully", Jack Fisher wrote in a letter to Lord Esher at the time. "He told me he would die in his boots. So he has. And a Fine Death......He was an exploder of gas bags and the terror of liars".

Brocklehurst and Stead, despite their differences of background and opinions, had remained firm friends since their first meeting with Charles Gordon in 1884, and their exchange of letters was delightfully 'full of high spirits and chaff'.

Several of them were on military matters and some concerned unfortunate soldiers who had applied to Stead for help regarding their personal grievances or ill-luck - some genuine, some humbugs. Brocklehurst always inquired into these and reported back to Stead in full. "Please don't mind writing to me about things like this", he wrote. "I will always do what I can."

Latterly there were some particularly vituperative letters from Brocklehurst about Lord Gladstone, W E Gladstone's youngest son, who had been made Governor-General of the Union of South Africa in 1910. "Is that sublime ass Gladstone to be recalled, or are we to have another Owen Lanyon with a black rising as a reward? I am told that Lady G 'don't know where she are' considers herself Royalty and expects Homage. "If Lord

G stops the least he can do is to put her out on some lonely farm, 20 miles from help ....".

In a later letter he complains that "Gladstone as far as I can judge deliberately trod on the best corn of the whole of the white population of S.A. just to show his power and importance, and it was the act of a conceited ass - If you don't know the feeling of the white population in S.A. on this particular point (assault of nigger on white woman) well I do. If Gladstone does not know he is not fit for his post. If he has strong ideas as to capital punishment, well and good, but in that case he should never have been appointed. Forgive warmth, but this business has fairly made me boil and anyway you can't accuse me of being agin the Govt," Brocklehurst commented.

Stead himself had never been afraid of tackling difficult and entrenched issues and had not only been styled 'lecturer-general' to the Tsar of Russia, but was also inclined to influence his own sovereign. "I have read Mr Stead's article in his ' Review of Reviews' - so sent it on to the King to read", Queen Alexandra wrote in a letter to Brocklehurst. "I thought it very good tell him so from me!! But *entre nous* rather condescending & patronizing telling him what to do next!!!"

He had even had the temerity to tell the Tsar, when he met him in Russia, that it would have done him "a world of good" to have served a term in jail as Stead himself had done.

Brocklehurst appears to have had some sympathy with Stead's spiritualism and his investigations into parapsychology, although he had been known to joke on the eve of a race meeting "You haven't by chance got a Spook who knows what is going to win tomorrow.?"

Stead's daughter Estelle in her biography *My Father* mentions that Brocklehurst attended the Gordon seance which Stead held and Brocklehurst's eldest sister, Maimie Bayley-Worthington, appears to have been equally interested in spiritual matters and to have funded Julia's Bureau (for spiritualism) after Stead's death, when it was called The W T Stead Bureau and operated from 1914 to 1936.

Brocklehurst continued his friendship with Stead's family and was Chairman of the Stead Hostel Committee to run the Hostels which were established as a living memorial to Stead.

He would also have been among the 2,500 people who attended Stead's memorial service at the Westminster Chapel to mourn the loss of his wittiest and most intelligent friend.

CHAPTER EIGHTEEN

As the war clouds gathered across Europe Brocklehurst was among the many old soldiers who were concerned at Britain's unprepared state for war. With the loss of Stead he was deprived of the means to get his views into print, but whenever he had the chance to speak in public he was an outspoken critic of the government's disregard of the lack of military training and strongly urged the neccessity of universal military service.

In the opening years of the war he was quick to add actions to his words and threw himself at once into a strenuous recruiting campaign in Rutland, where he was Lord Lieutenant. He had already been responsible for raising two companies of territorials and in 1908 had been appointed Hon Colonel of the 5th Battalion Leicester Regiment - the Volunteer Battalion.

At a time when the landed gentry were trained to use guns from an early age in pursuit of sport, but this privilege did not extend to the majority of young men, he had established miniature Rifle Ranges at Oakham and Uppingham and took an active part in the formation of village Rifle Clubs throughout his home sphere of Rutland and Leicestershire. At the Oakham Long Rifle Club he offered a silver cup, value £10 to be shot for annually and local history records that 'it was owing to the support and financial assistance readily given by him that these movements for training men to shoot were so very successful.'

While the Army had been ill-prepared for war, the Navy was in fine shape, thanks to the efforts of Jack Fisher, who had been able to carry through his reforms for the service before retiring in 1910. However, in October 1914 Churchill, supported by Asquith, proposed recalling Fisher as First Sea Lord. King George V, who detested Fisher as much as his father had liked him, opposed the move, but Churchill succeeded in recalling him and together he and Fisher 'generated an energy and enthusiasm that made the Admiralty hum with confidence'.

Fisher was quick to let his friend Brocklehurst know the good news:

"My Beloved Friend"

You must come and lunch with us very often with your dear wife when we get into the Admiralty in a few days time. <u>I have some lovely stories for you!!!.</u> Here is one. "When the King said to Winston and the Prime Minister (to dissuade them) that the job would kill me - Winston instantly replied 'Sir, I cannot imagine a more glorious death'. Queen Alexandra and Princess Victoria simply heavenly to me and they both looked quite lovely. I wish I could have married both of them."

Despite his 74 years Fisher set out with immense energy on an enormous shipbuilding programme. "Such an Armada - a veritable Armada it is - has never in the memory of man or the annals of the world been devised and constructed in so short a time.....every one of them new in type and revolutionary in design and all worked out for a specific strategic idea."

Unfortunately the Fisher and Churchill partnership lasted for barely six months until Fisher resigned over Churchill's plan to send a fleet to force a naval passage through the Dardanelles in order to capture Constantinople and so relieve the pressure which Turkey (Germany's ally) was exerting over Russia. Fisher believed that British sea power in wartime should be concentrated in home waters.

With his customary flamboyance he resigned on the 15th May 1915, announcing that he was off to Scotland "so as to avoid all questions". In fact he went to ground in the Charing Cross Hotel. After he received a note from Asquith, saying "In the King's name I order you to remain at your post" he postponed his departure to Scotland, although he refused to return to the Admiralty, even though Queen Alexandra had written him an impassioned letter begging him to stay - "Stick to your post like Nelson.....let the young foolhardy one (Churchill) go."

Fisher later apologised to the King for his departure, but for the remainder of the war he continued to be at the centre of political controversy and his correspondence with Brocklehurst refers to documents which he must not on any account show to the King - particularly his letters to Asquith, which had been suppressed. He was also concerned with the "damnable intrigue to withdraw Admiral Jellico (his protege) from the Grand Fleet just to spite me! (so I'm told)."

In 1917 Fisher complained to Brocklehurst that he was being "plagued by interviews, but I see no-one. If I did see anyone do you know what I would say to the interviewer - 'Sir, Do you think I should have got the Order of Merit unless I had been persistently maligned?' He ended the letter with "Love to Louisa please!" A friend had beseeched him to go about buttonholing people everywhere. "Yesterday I was asked to meet a mass of journalists at dinner, but I declined", he told Brocklehurst. "I really don't think it's dignified to be knocking at the back door and trying to get in that way! I'm quite well known. I can waltz 12 waltzes without stopping and I can say the Lord's Prayer backwards!. What more do you want???. Fond love to Louisa".

This dispute was played against a Court which had become increasingly more austere and spartan to meet the war effort. Balmoral was closed and the Court repaired to Windsor Castle, which became teetotal when Lloyd George, who had succeeded Asquith as Prime Minister after a political coup, suggested to the King that the Royal Family should set an example to the public by giving up alcohol for the duration of the war.

The bleakest year of the war for Britain and its allies was 1917 when Russia collapsed in two revolutions and signed an Armistice with Germany and the Central Powers.

Brocklehurst heard from Queen Alexandra of the trials of her sister, the Dowager Empress of Russia during the October Revolution..

She had been very ill "in consequence of that awful night visit of those brutal revolutionists - who dragged her out of bed - made her sit by her bed side with nothing on but a dressingown & bare feet for 4 hours while they searched through every drawer in her two little rooms & took away all her favorite things even letters from her dead husband & her prayer books fr. her Parents too infamous really-during this time while a dozen of these brutes were in her room -her maid & her two remaining Cossacks were also shut up & arrested - no wonder she caught cold - & & think of all she went through & had to bear with such really wonderful courage & pluck - But it really is too horrible to think of & all she has to bear & go through besides the terrible anxiety about her Children - She is at present staying near her two daughters & families and this is the 50th year of her life in Russia which she loved so deeply & devoted her whole life to. Oh it is all too dreadfully sad and I confess the anxiety about her makes me quite ill & miserable", she wrote.

Brocklehurst's own family were actively engaged in the war. His nephew Jack, his brother Harry's eldest son, a Captain in the Coldstream Guards, had been among the first troops to land in France in 1914. After being wounded twice in the first year of the war he was transferred to the Sudan, perhaps at Brocklehurst's suggestion and served in the Egyptian Army there from 1916 to 1920. Brocklehurst's niece, Marjorie died from typhoid en route to visit her husband Viscount Quenington in the Egyptian War in 1916, and he was killed in battle a month later. Two of his cousins, Sir Philip Brocklehurst and his brother, Courtney, were in the trenches in France until Sir Philip was seriously wounded and Courtney left the 10th Royal Hussars to join the Royal Flying Corps - the forerunner of the Royal Air Force.

As an experienced regimental officer Brocklehurst knew how important it was to look after the families of the men on active service and one of his first moves on the outbreak of hostilities had been to reconstitute the Rutland Soldiers and Sailors Families' Association . He very actively supported the King George's Fund for Sailors, the VAD Hospital and the Red Cross and was President of the County Committee for War Savings.

Ernest Walker, who was a pupil at Langham School at the time remembers the General coming into the classroom one day and telling the whole senior school that he would start any girl or boy with a first issue War Savings Certificate, value 16 shillings (80p) if they learnt and recited to the headmaster the 13th chapter of St.Paul's Epistle to the Corinthians ["Though I speak with the tongues of men and angels"] within a stated time. Not many of the children, including Ernest, learnt the lines in time, but Margaret Catchpole was among those who did and when I met her at Langham recently she repeated them to me word perfect although she is now more than 90-years-old. Together with Audrey Hubbard and Benjie Walker she remembered the General as a very tall, God-fearing gentleman with a large drooping cavalry moustache - now quite white with age.

Although Brocklehurst was Lord Lieutenant of the county, and with his great height a commanding figure locally, he and Louie were outranked in Rutland during the hunting season by the Lonsdales at nearby Barleythorpe Hall. From his seat in the choir stalls Ernest Walker recalls Lord and Lady Lonsdale arriving at the church in an open landau drawn by four black horses, with a coachman and postilion. The landau was painted in his lordship's special Chinese yellow. No ordinary coach painter or wheelwright was ever allowed to daub his version of the colour on any of his vehicles. Only "Lordy's" own painter knew the special colour formula and the secret of the 'mix'. The coachman and postilion were resplendent in black frock-tailed coats and Chinese yellow cardigans - white buckskin trousers, and black silk top hats with black and yellow cockades. As if by arrangement the Lonsdales always arrived at the church last, just as the service was about to start (or should have started). The Ranksboroughs would have arrived a few minutes earlier in their more modest hansom cab.

Rutland at that time was still a mainly agricultural county. Although horses held first place in Brocklehurst's affections he also became known as a cattle breeder with herds of Shorthorns, Dexter Kerries and Aberdeen Angus on his Ranksborough acres. The Rutland Agricultural Society enjoyed his interest as its one-time president and generous patron.

Langham village then consisted of many smallholdings, each having two to six cow commons. A youth was paid 40 shillings a year to fetch the cattle to the gate, morning and evening for the milkers, and presumably to keep him and the waiting milkers amused Brocklehurst had a skittle bed built at the gate entrance.

It was a relief to escape to the comparative quiet of the countryside from the clamours and sorrows of the war. As he wrote to Queen Alexandra to report on yet another Memorial Service this time for their friend Colonel Franks she replied: "It is terribly sad to think how many a splendid life has been lost both of Officers & Men in this terribly cruel & awful war! but God be thanked we are nearing the end - thanks to _our_ glorious Army under our **great** General Haig & our brave Allies. Soon the Culprit the Hun Emperor will get his well deserved punishment.

Jack Fisher appeared to be still courting political controversy - claiming that as he had not heard from Brocklehurst for some time he thought he had boycotted him - "How about Queen Alexandra is she savage and Princess Victoria RSVP - I don't care about the Rest! As I'm in all the Pantomimes I suppose I'm all right!!! There'll be a clear out before long!" he hoped.

Brocklehurst's cousin, John Fielden wrote rejoicing that "the Germans have got served out for their sins, if we only keep them to the Peace Terms and don't let them off any of them, but I fear President Wilson is inclined to be too kind-hearted. Perhaps his trip to the Fighting Line will open his eyes a little as to what they have done" Fielden predicted Industrial War in England and regretted the policy of "giving way to every body that strikes" which was simply "bribery for election purposes". Finally he queried why soldiers in England who had work waiting for them should not be demobilised at once. "It is simply hopeless to try and get a man back, unless you have Private Influence, which has been the curse of this War and has kept hundreds of men out of the Army. At the present rate - Demobilisation will go on for years!" he complained.

There are no records which show that Brocklehurst was ever a member of the Government and presumably as Lord-in-Waiting to the King this would not have been possible, but among his papers a letter from Lloyd-George dated 3rd January 1919 says

"In view of the recent general election and of the termination of the war, I have advised the King that a reconstruction of the Government is necessary and His Majesty has given his consent.

I should be greatly obliged if you would place your resignation in my hands in order to enable me to submit the name of a new Ministry to His Majesty."

There are reports to him from Stead's son Alfred from the Salonica front in 1917 which suggest Brocklehurst may have been advising at the War Office but nothing more so this letter is a puzzle. He was still at the time of his death, Lord-in-Waiting to the King and Extra Equerry to Queen Alexandra.

CHAPTER NINETEEN

Brocklehurst was in his 70th year when he died at Ranksborough Hall, fittingly perhaps, on the 28th February 1921 - the anniversary of the relief of Ladysmith. A letter from Queen Mary to Queen Alexandra on that day says "We are much distressed at the sad death of dear Lord Ranksborough, and knowing what an old friend of yours he was, I must send you a line of sympathy at the loss of one who was so devoted to you and such a good kind friend.

It appears that after having been desperately ill he took a decided turn for the better yesterday & they were all quite happy about him so that the news of his death [from pneumonia] came as a great shock. All this we heard from his nice sister Lady Fitzwilliam who is broken hearted at his death."

"He gave faithful service to God, King and Country and was Greatly Beloved by all" was how his widow Louie wished him to be remembered, as letters and tributes poured in from around the country, including one from Queen Alexandra saying "how deeply I feel for you & share yr deep Grief and sorrow. You must indeed feel so terribly sad & lonely without that devoted & best of husbands. I always looked upon him as one of my dearest & oldest of friends & shall never cease to regret him".

In the Household Brigade Magazine Lord Erroll wrote an

obituary notice for "BROCK" with whom he had served for over twenty years in the Blues, both as a subaltern and later as his Commanding Officer.

"I should say his chief characteristic was his intensely human outlook and the sympathetic standpoint from which he approached all questions concerning the welfare of his fellow-men. His altruism was spontaneous and disinterested. It came somehow natural to him to look at things from the point of view of our common humanity." he wrote.   " As a young man he came for a time under the influence of General Gordon and never lost the faith with which the latter inspired him. His religion was very real, unostentatious, and always practical in its application.   As a friend, he was kindly, true and cheery, a charming companion, and a trusty comrade. He was the ideal of a cavalry soldier, a perfect horseman, a *beau sabreur* in every sense, and a very gallant gentleman to boot.....There are few men who occupied so unique a position among his contemporaries or will be more missed among a large circle of friends".

Following the example of his Aunt Emma, and at a time when it was becoming to be considered less barbaric, Brocklehurst had left instructions for his body to be cremated - even though the nearest crematorium was at Golders Green. To complete his final journey his coffin went by train from Oakham to St Pancras where it was met by 'a detachment of the old Regiment he loved so well who carried him to his last resting place.'

On the same day two memorial services were held. The first at noon in the Chapel Royal , St James's Palace, attended by a distinguished company and many members of the Royal household. The King was represented by Lord Stanmore, Queen Alexandra by Colonel Sir Arthur Davidson, the King and Queen of Norway by Mr C A Ponsonby and Princess Christian by Mr Hugo Wemyss.

The second was held at Langham and has been described as 'the greatest spectacle ever witnessed in the village'. Ernest Walker from his place in the choir has left a remarkable eye-witness account of the ceremony 'the arrangements for which were made by Buckingham Palace officials, with due consultation with Lady Ranksborough, whose husband had been held in so high esteem by all at 'the Palace'.

'The day and date of the Memorial Service being fixed (no doubt to suit those of Royal blood who intended to be present), and the venue being the parish church of St Peter & St Paul, Langham, preparations were put in hand.' he recalled. ' So far as I was concerned as a Choir Boy, three special choir practices were arranged. The first one revealed the order of service - hymns and psalms to be sung - and our resident organist was at the church organ.   The following two practices were taken entirely by Dr.Malcolm Sargent (later Sir Malcolm then organist at Melton Mowbray, where the Prince of Wales had his hunting lodge - Craven Cottage.) Dr Malcolm Sargent really put us through our paces for the two successive evenings prior to the service. I recall practising 'Fight the Good Fight' (after all Lord Ranksborough was primarily a soldier) - through no less than five times'.

Another hymn chosen 'Nearer my God to thee 'was said to have been played by the ship's orchestra as the *Titanic* went down and would have reminded Brocklehurst of his friend Stead, who was a victim of the disaster. The psalm chosen was 'I will lift up my eyes unto the hills'. These hymns and psalm were supposed to have been his favourites.

'Meanwhile strange saloon cars with liveried chauffeurs and other large vans from London arrived and departed,' Ernest recalled. ' Rolls and rolls of Royal blue carpet were deposited in the church and laid wherever carpet could be laid, and then finally on the appointed afternoon, first came the floral tributes, some of immense size and composed of exotic flowers, from the King and Queen, Queen Alexandra, the War Office and so on. Two large railway vans containing wreaths had been detached from a London express at Oakham, it was said. Other mourners brought their own floral tributes with them.

Liveried Gentlemen-at-Arms conducted each mourner to his appointed place. Behind Lady Ranksborough and other chief mourners sat the Prince of Wales, representing the King, beside him, his brother George, Duke of York. Behind them Sir Douglas (afterwards Lord) Haig, Chief of Staff War Office and other senior officers and with and behind them Dukes, Marquesses, Earls, Lords, Ladies and Gentlemen, many in uniform, from all over the realm. It is doubtful if such a distinguished company has ever gathered in a village church at any time.

Doctor Sargent, complete with his academic ermine stole, was seated at the organ, which had been specially tuned at short notice following our first choir practice with him! The Vicar at the time was the Rev Mandle MA Oxon. The choir processed from the vestry at the west end of the church whilst the doctor played something unknown to me - The Dead March from Saul - and we took our places in the choir stalls. The hymn 'Fight the Good Fight' was sung, followed by some prayers and the psalm, after which the inevitable 13th Chapter of St Paul's Epistle to the Corinthians was read by Sir Douglas Haig - whilst I thought about the sixteen shillings Savings Certificate which I had narrowly missed receiving at school a few years previously when I failed to learn this chapter in the prescribed time.   The Choir then led the procession from the church to the War Memorial outside, where it had been agreed the ceremony of laying the wreaths would take place. The scene that followed was almost a replica of the present Remembrance procedure at the Cenotaph, except that the much smaller village memorial could not contain the vast number of tributes which covered the plinth and paved surround, and still there were tributes to be laid on the adjacent grass bank.

Two six-foot trumpeters from the Horse Guards rendered 'The Last Post' followed by 'Reveille' - a prayer was said and we led the way back into the church where the hymn 'Nearer my God to Thee' was sung followed by the Blessing . Then the choir withdrew to the vestry to the sound of an organ voluntary which we choirboys afterwards said 'might have burst the bellows of the organ' such was the volume. The Service was now at its end and the mourners departed. The Prince of Wales following the chief mourners and so on in order of rank until the church was empty. Outside the village streets and square were packed with the cars of all who had attended and it was more than an hour before the village returned to normal and some weeks later before the last of the withered floral tributes were carted to the village refuse tip.'

As Brocklehurst had no heir the Ranksborough title died with him. His widow, Louie remained at Ranksborough Hall until her death in 1936 but the staff was reduced and the distinguished visitors no longer came. Never again will the large entrance hall at Ranksborough echo with the sound of hand bells or the voices of the church choir with their Christmas carols. Like Barleythorpe Hall and so many other great houses it has passed to owners and users of another age and purpose.

A marble tablet in Brocklehurst's memory was erected by Louie on the north side of the chancel in the parish church of St Peter & St Paul at Langham, although due to disrepair his regimental pennant no longer hangs beside it. His ashes were moved from the Columbarium at Golders Green sometime after his funeral and placed in the Brocklehurst family vault in St Mary's Church at Sudeley Castle, where there is also a plaque in his memory, listing his military and Royal honours. It concludes with the words 'a devoted friend to General Gordon'. Whoever chose the inscription, and it was probably his brother Harry, knew how important that last designation would have been to him.

Author's Note

Primary Sources

The Ranksborough Papers
Sudeley Castle Archives

Royal Archives

RA VIC/T8/149 28 August 1884 p.81
RA VIC/023/64A 10 November 1884p.92
RA VIC/T9/14 15 February 1885 p.113
RA VIC/QVJ 5 July 1899 p.125
RA VIC/E 33/75 p.127
RA VIC/QVJ/1899 6-7 November p.134
RA VIC/QVJ/1900: 3 March p.136
RA VIC/ P7/49 8 May 1900 p.137
RA VIC/P10/62 12 June 1900 p.137
RA VIC/QVJ/1900:27 November p.142
RA VIC/W 47/277 pp.159,160
RA PS/GV/O2548/38 28 February 1921 p.183

Churchill Archives Centre
Churchill College Cambridge S/1.10
Letters from Brocklehurst to WT Stead

BIBLIOGRAPHY

Writings by Gordon
Letters of General CG Gordon to His Sister M A Gordon
[edited by Augusta Gordon] Macmillan 1888
Journal of Major-General CG Gordon CB at Kartoum
Edited by A Egmont Hake Kegan Paul & Trench 1885

Other Published Sources
Battiscombe Georgina *Queen Alexandra* Constable
Bond Brian *Victorian Military Campaigns* Hutchinson 1967
Crozier Mary *An Old Silk Family* 1745-1945 Aberdeen University Press 1947
Cust Lionel *King Edward VII and his Court* Murray 1930
Edwards Amelia B Edwards *A Thousand Miles Up the Nile* Century Publishing 1982
Farwell Byron *For Queen and Country* Allen Lane 1981
Flint John *Cecil Rhodes* Hutchinson 1976
Giddings Robert Imperial Echoes Leo Cooper
Healey Edna *Lady Unknown - the Life of Angela Burdett-Coutts* Sidgwick & Jackson 1978
Hill R.*Biographical Dictionary of the Sudan* Oxford Clarendon Press 1967
Inwood Stephen *The History of London* Macmillan 1998
Longford Elizabeth *Victoria RI*
Magnus Philip *King Edward VII* 1964
Marder Arthur J. *Fear God and Dread Nought* Cape
Maurice F and G Arthur *The Life of Lord Wolseley* Heinemann 1924
Moorehead Alan *The White Nile* Hamish Hamilton 1960
Pakenham Thomas *The Boer War* George Weidenfeld & Nicholson 1985
Pollock John *Gordon -The Man Behind the Legend* Constable
Rose Kenneth *King George V* Weidenfeld & Nicholson
            Kings Queens & Courtiers Weidenfeld & Nicholson 1985
Steevens GW *With Kitchener to Khartoum* 1898
Strachey Lytton *Eminent Victorians* Oxford University Press 2003
Symons Julian *Buller's Campaign* Cresset Press 1963
Sutherland Douglas *The Yellow Earl - the Life of Hugh Lowther 5th Earl Lonsdale* Cassell 1965
Thompson Brian *Imperial Vanities* Harper Collins 2001
Whyte Frederic *The Life of WT Stead* Jonathan Cape 1925
Wilson A N *The Victorians* Hutchinson 2002

Articles and Monographs
Baylen Joseph O *W T Stead and the Boer War:The Irony of Idealism*

The Canadian Historical Review 1959
 WT Stead's History of the Mystery and the Jameson Raid
The Journal of British Studies,Trinity College, Connecticut 1964
The Tsar's "Lecturer-General"
WT Stead and the Russian Revolution of 1905
Research Paper No 23 July 1969 Georgia State College,
Atlanta, Georgia.
Gerald Graham's *Last Words with Gordon* Littels Living Age February 19 1897
Stead William T
Christian Commonwealth Publishing Co.1897

INDEX

Jean Bray

Jean Bray has been a writer and journalist for more than forty years, starting her career in Africa. She came to London to work on The Daily Herald and has since contributed news and features to a wide variety of publications, as well as producing and editing corporate newspapers and magazines. She is now researching and updating the archives at Sudeley Castle and lives with her artist husband in Winchcombe.